TECH*Knits*

First published in Great Britain in 2013
by Bloomsbury Publishing Plc
50 Bedford Square
London WC1B 3DP

www.bloomsbury.com

© Copyright Quid Publishing 2012

ISBN 978-1-4725-0473-9

Printed in China

Conceived, designed and produced by
Quid Publishing
Level 4, Sheridan House
112-114 Western Road
Hove, BN3 1DD
United Kingdom

Design by Clare Barber

TECH *Knits*

FROM RETRO ROBOTS TO SPACE ROCKETS:
20 Technology-Inspired Projects for Knitters

B L O O M S B U R Y
LONDON • NEW DELHI • NEW YORK • SYDNEY

Contents

INTRODUCTION

Tech Knits is a nostalgic collection of designs inspired by space and technology. Vintage shades and iconic symbols have been combined to create a range of exciting accessories for the home and to wear. Memories of sci-fi comic strips, old toys, and retro technology have been incorporated into the patterns, resulting in a collection with appeal for all ages.

The 20 projects are designed to suit a range of skill levels and provide a good introduction to working with colour and textures. Each pattern has been given a score from 1–100 to define the skill level needed – the lower the score, the easier the pattern.

Projects include a patchwork blanket covered with colourful rockets and glittering stars, a mobile of the planet Saturn surrounded by four moons, a sleek metallic flying saucer paperweight, and a pair of socks embellished with a radio mast. Each pattern has a tip box, offering useful hints and suggestions for changing sizes and colour. For novice knitters, there is a Basics section offering step-by-step instructions for getting started and including the various techniques used in the book. There is also a section on materials and equipment to help you choose the right tools.

The quantities given for materials throughout the book are based on average requirements and may vary. If using a substitute yarn, always check the tension and use larger or smaller needles if necessary to achieve the correct tension.

The Basics

The projects in this book include short-row shaping, Fair Isle, intarsia, beading, felting, cables and embroidery. (These methods are all explained in the techniques section.)

MATERIALS
and Equipment

YARN

Yarn comes in many different fibres and thicknesses.

Various fibres suit different projects. For the purposes of this book I have used mostly wool or cotton.

Pure wool is beautiful to handle, gives warmth and elasticity, and in some cases can be machine washed. There are luxurious blends of wool and cashmere or alpaca, which are soft and warm, and there are hard-wearing blends of wool and nylon, mostly used for socks.

Cotton is a versatile yarn; it is great for kids' knits as it washes well and is soft against the skin, it is also a good choice for home accessories. Cotton denim is a very hard-wearing yarn that shrinks in length on the first wash closing up the stitches to make a dense fabric.

A ply is a single strand of fibre, and yarns will vary in structure depending on how they are plied. Some are twisted and some are cabled. Confusingly a thick yarn could have just one ply and a fine yarn could have eight plies. Ply is

also used when naming the weight (thickness or gauge) of yarn, usually the smaller the number the finer the yarn.

All yarns come in a different ply, and this can be determined by the needle size used and the tension or tension given in a pattern and on the ball band. Various terms are used in different countries, but this is a general guide.

❋ **LACE WEIGHT:** super-fine, 2-ply

❋ **4-PLY:** fine, 3-ply, 5-ply, baby

❋ **DK:** light, light worsted

❋ **ARAN:** medium, worsted

❋ **CHUNKY:** Bulky, craft, rug

❋ **SUPER CHUNKY:** Super Bulky, roving

If you want to substitute the yarn used in a pattern, always check the tension and knit a tension square.

KNITTING NEEDLES

Knitting needles are most commonly available in plastic, aluminium, wood, and bamboo. They are available in a set of sizes that range from 2mm to 25mm. A conversion chart is provided on page 140, which includes all the sizes. As a general rule the finer the yarn the smaller the needle. However, some lace weight yarns are knitted on larger needles to obtain a lacier effect.

Circular needles are popular for many projects. They are made up of two needle tips with a length of cord joining them. They can be used for knitting in the round or backward and forward like a straight needle.

Double-pointed needles come in sets of four or five and are used for knitting in the round; usually for small items such as socks, sleeves, hats, and gloves. They are also used for knitting i-cords.

Crochet hooks come in a similar size range to knitting needles. They are generally shorter than knitting needles, with a hooked end. A few of the projects in this book require basic crochet edging.

Circuit Board Scarf, page 84

ACCESSORIES

The most useful accessories for general projects are:

* **STITCH HOLDER:** A giant safety pin to hold stitches that are not being worked.

* **ROW COUNTER:** A small plastic tally that keeps count of the rows. This is very useful when working from a chart or knitting complicated lace patterns.

* **CABLE NEEDLE:** A short double-pointed needle used for cable work (see page 14).

* **TAPESTRY NEEDLE:** A needle for sewing up with a blunt end and large eye.

* **STITCH MARKERS:** Plastic markers used to mark a stitch pattern or end of round.

* **TAPE MEASURE:** Useful in metric and imperial measurements.

* **SCISSORS:** A small pair of scissors.

* **BEADING NEEDLE:** A long, fine sewing needle for threading beads.

Techniques

CASTING ON

CABLE CAST-ON

Make a slipknot and place it on the left-hand needle.

Insert the right-hand needle in the slipknot, pass the yarn around the needle as if you are knitting a stitch, draw the loop through and place it on the left-hand needle.

Place the right-hand needle between the two stitches, pass the yarn around the needle, pull the loop through and place it on the left-hand needle.

Repeat stage three, always placing the right-hand needle between the two stitches nearest the tip. Continue until you have sufficient stitches.

LONG-TAIL CAST-ON

Holding the needle in your right hand, measure out a tail of yarn roughly three times the length of the edge to be cast on. Make a slipknot and place it on the needle.

Wrap the tail end over your thumb, place the tip of the needle under the yarn at the front of your thumb, and knit a stitch by passing the ball end of the yarn over the needle.

Continue until you have sufficient stitches.

CASTING OFF

BASIC CAST-OFF

Knit two stitches, then pass the first stitch knitted over the stitch closest to the tip of the needle.

Knit the next stitch on the left-hand needle, then pass the first stitch on the right-hand needle over the stitch just knitted.

Continue to the end of the row until you have one stitch remaining; cut the yarn, pass the yarn end through the remaining stitch, and draw tight.

THREE-NEEDLE CAST-OFF

This is used for joining two pieces of knitting, often used at a shoulder seam or for any project that needs a ridged edging.

Place the two pieces of knitting wrong sides together, holding the two knitting needles in the left hand with the points facing the same way. Insert the tip of the right-hand needle into the first stitch on each of the left-hand needles, knit these two stitches together and place the new stitch on the right-hand needle.

Insert the tip of the right-hand needle into the first stitch on each of the left-hand needles, knit these two stitches together and place the new stitch on the right-hand needle.

Pass the first stitch on the right-hand needle over the stitch just knitted.

Continue to the end of the row until you have a neat ridge of cast-off stitches and one stitch remaining. Cut the yarn and pass the end through the remaining stitch and draw tight.

COMMON STITCHES

The following are the main stitches needed for knitting:

KNIT STITCH

Place the tip of the right-hand needle in the first stitch on the left-hand needle, going in through from left to right.

Taking the yarn behind the right-hand needle, bring it through between the two needle-tips and pull the loop through with the right-hand needle.

This loop on the right-hand needle is the new stitch. Drop the original loop from the left-hand needle.

Continue working in this way to the end of the row, when all the stitches are on the right-hand needle.

PURL STITCH

Bring the yarn to the front of the work. Insert the right-hand needle tip in the first stitch on the left-hand needle from right to left.

Wrap the yarn between the two needle tips and around to the front of the right-hand needle.

Pull the loop through onto the right-hand needle to make a stitch and let the loop drop from the left-hand needle.

Continue working in this way to the end of the row so all the stitches are on the right-hand needle.

STOCKING STITCH

This is a smooth stitch with a right side and a wrong side, and is formed by working one row in knit and one row in purl. The knit side is always the right side of the work.

REVERSED STOCKING STITCH

This is exactly the same as stocking stitch but the purl side is always the right side of the work.

GARTER STITCH

This is a ridged stitch that will not curl at the edges and is suitable for borders and scarves. It is formed by working every row in the knit stitch.

Flying Saucer Paperweight, page 42

RIB

An elastic border that is mostly used for welts and cuffs on garments.

K1, P1 RIB: K1, p1. With the yarn at the back of work, knit 1 stitch, bring the yarn to the front of work and purl 1 stitch. These two stitches are repeated to the end of the row. The next row will start as follows: If you ended the previous row with K1, begin this row with P1. If you ended the previous row with P1, begin this row with K1

K2, P2 RIB. K2, p2. With the yarn at the back of work, knit 2 stitches, bring the yarn to the front of work, purl 2 stitches. Repeat to the end of the row. The next row will start as follows: If you ended the previous row with k2, begin this row with p2. If you ended the previous row with p2, begin this row with k2

MOSS STITCH

This forms a textured stitch that will not curl.

ROW 1: Work as a k1, p1 rib to the end of row

ROW 2: If you ended the previous row with k1, begin this row with k1. If you ended the previous row with p1, begin this row with p1

CABLE

There are various methods of cabling and special abbreviations will be given in individual patterns. It is a method of crossing the stitches to form a textured design. A number of stitches are placed on a cable needle and held at the back or front of work. Knit a similar number of stitches from the left-hand needle, then knit the stitches from the cable needle.

BEADING

Thread sufficient beads on to the yarn before casting on. Thread a fine sewing or beading needle with sewing thread, tie the ends of the thread to form a loop. Place the end of the knitting yarn through this loop, thread the beads onto the needle and push down on to the knitting yarn. Continue until enough beads have been threaded to complete the design.

When indicated to place a bead on the knitting, bring the yarn with a bead to the front of work, push the bead so that it is tight against the needle, slip the next stitch, take the yarn to the back of work and knit the next stitch.

FAIR ISLE

Fair Isle is a method of working in colour by weaving the yarn not in use at the back of the work. The colours are changed every 2–4 stitches and there are usually no more than two or three different colours to a row.

INTARSIA

Intarsia is a method of working large blocks of colour. To stop tangles forming, small lengths of yarn are wound off onto bobbins. When a colour is changed, the yarns are crossed at the back of the work to prevent a hole forming.

GRAFTING

This forms an invisible seam between two pieces of knitting along an edge that would otherwise have been cast off.

Lay the two pieces of knitting with the edges to be grafted meeting and right side facing up. Thread a needle with the knitting yarn, slip a few stitches at a time off the knitting needle and pass the sewing needle through the stitches from each piece to form a row of stitches.

MATTRESS ST

This forms an invisible seam up the side edge of two pieces of knitting.

Lay the two pieces of knitting with the edges to be sewn meeting and RS facing up. Thread a needle with the knitting yarn and attach. Place the needle under the bar of the first stitch on the right-hand piece of knitting, then under the bar of the first stitch on the left-hand piece of knitting, continue up the seam weaving in and out of the stitches in this way then pull the thread tight.

TASSELS

Used to embellish scarves, hats and cushions.

Wind 10 strands of yarn around a piece of card. Cut through one end of the loops. Keeping the loops folded in half, use a crochet hook to pull the folded end through the knitting. Pass the cut ends through the loop and pull tight.

FELTING

Knitted pieces can be put in the washing machine and washed on a high temperature to matt the fibres. This produces a strong dense fabric. Always use a yarn that is known to felt, such as a pure wool that should be hand

Calculator Tablet Cover, page 118

washed or a wool and alpaca blend. It is advisable to wash on a medium temperature the first time to avoid too much shrinkage. The item can be washed again at a higher temperature if necessary.

SHORT-ROW SHAPING

A method of shaping that will create a curve in the edge of the knitting. It is useful for collars or creating circular pieces of knitting. Part of a row is knitted, the work is then turned and worked back to the beginning.

DOUBLE-KNIT METHOD

This creates a double-sided piece of fabric using two shades.

Cast on the amount of stitches required using two strands of yarn.

Knit the first stitch with the corresponding colour, bring both strands to the front of work and purl the second stitch with the corresponding colour. Continue to the end of the row.

Repeat this row throughout taking care not to twist the stitches.

Atomic Laptop Cover, page 30

CHAIN STITCH

An embroidery stitch used for embellishment.

Thread a needle with the required yarn.

Bring the needle up through to the front of the fabric, then back down the same hole, leaving a small loop.

Bring the needle back up through the loop securing it in place.

Continue in this way until you have a chain of stitches.

FRENCH KNOT

Thread a needle with the required yarn.

Bring the needle up through the front of the fabric.

Wrap the yarn around the needle as many times as you want.

Bring the needle back through the fabric pushing the knot tightly.

SINGLE CROCHET

Place the crochet hook in the next stitch, pull a loop of yarn through, wrap the yarn around the crochet hook and pull through the loop on the hook. Repeat to the end of the row.

SWISS DARNING

This can be used as an alternative to Fair Isle or intarsia and is worked on the knit side of the fabric. You are basically covering the knitted stitch with another 'pretend' knitted stitch in a different colour.

Thread a needle with a contrasting shade to the main colour.

Bring the needle up through the work at the base of the stitch you are covering.

Pass the needle through the base of the stitch on the row above.

Bring the needle back down through the base of the original stitch.

Abbreviations

ALT – alternate

BEG – beginning

CM – centimetre

CN – cable needle

CO – cast off

CONT – continue

DEC – decrease

DPN – double-pointed needle

FOLL – following, follows

G – gram

G-ST – garter stitch

IN(S) – inch(es)

INC – including

K – knit

K2TOG – knit 2 together

KWISE – knitwise

M1 – make 1; pick up the loop lying between st on LH needle and stitch on RH needle and knit into the back of it

MM – millimetre

P – purl

PATT – pattern

PSSO – pass slip st over

PWISE – purlwise

REM – remaining

REP – repeat

RS – right side

SKP – sl1, k1, pass slip st over

SL – slip

ST ST – stocking stitch

ST(S) – stitch(es)

TBL – through back of loop

TOG – together

W1 – wrap 1; with yarn at front of work sl next st from RH needle to LH needle, take the yarn to the back of work, sl the st back to RH needle.

WS – wrong side

WYF – with yarn in front

YD – yards

YFWD – yarn forward

YON – yarn over needle

YRN – yarn round needle

CROCHET

CH – chain

SC – single crochet

SL ST – slip st

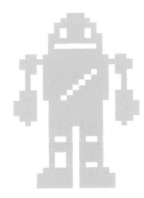

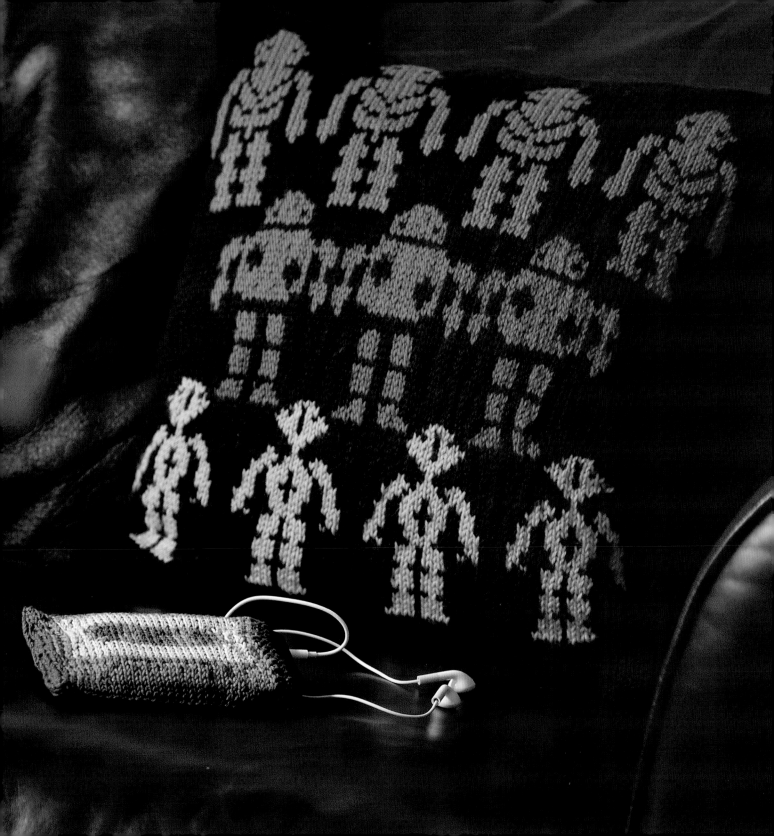

The Projects

The designs can be used to brighten up your home, and also make perfect gifts. You can adapt them to suit any colour scheme, and can add personal touches to your project with unusual buttons and embellishments.

GRAPHIC EQUALIZER
Scarf

A Graphic Equalizer is a classic symbol for any muso, the characteristic bands of colour determining the frequency response controlled by the slides. The graphic image lends itself perfectly to a knitting design and any budding musician would be proud to wear this striking scarf. It is the perfect image for a project like this, knitted in easy garter stitch and using the intarsia method to create bold blocks of colour. The extra long scarf is knitted from side to side on circular needles.

MATERIALS

YARN: Aran weight.

Shown here: Debbie Bliss Cashmerino Aran (55% merino wool, 33% microfibre, 12% cashmere; 90m (98yd)/50g): black (A), 4 balls; red (B), orange (C) and green (D), 1 ball each.

NEEDLES: 5mm: 100cm circular. Adjust needle size if necessary to obtain the correct tension.
HABERDASHERY: Tapestry needle.

TENSION: 18 sts and 34 rows to 10cm (4") in garter st using 5mm needles.

FINISHED SIZE:
About 14cm (5½") wide x 203cm (80") long.

PATTERN Note

When you knit each separate block of colour, weave in the tail end at the back of work as you are knitting. This will give a neat finish and save time on the sewing up when the knitting is finished.

SCARF

Using shade A, cast on 360 sts and working in garter st (all rows knit) throughout, continue as foll:

Work 4 rows in garter st.

ROW 5 (RS): K30 shade B, k2 shade A, k10 shade C, k2 shade A, k5 shade D, k265 shade A, k12 shade D, k2 shade A, k10 shade C, k2 shade A, k20 shade B.

ROW 6: K20 shade B, k2, shade A, k10 shade C, k2 shade A, k12 shade D, k265 shade A, k5 shade D, k2 shade A, k10 shade C, k2 shade A, k30 shade B.

ROWS 7 & 8: Rep rows 5 & 6 working colours as set on the row below.

ROWS 9 & 10: Using shade A, knit to end.

ROW 11: K48 shade B, k2 shade A, k8 shade C, k2 shade A, k4 shade D, k236 shade A, k10 shade D, k2 shade A, k10 shade C, k2 shade A, k36 shade B.

ROWS 12, 13 & 14: Work colours as set on the row below.

ROWS 15 & 16: Using shade A, knit to end.

ROW 17: K36 shade B, k2 shade A, k8 shade C, k2 shade A, k4 shade D, k240 shade A, k6 shade D, k2 shade A, k10 shade C, k2 shade A, k48 shade B.

ROWS 18, 19 & 20: Work colours as set on the row above.

ROWS 21 & 22: Using shade A, knit to end.

ROW 23: K34 shade B, k2 shade A, k6 shade C, k2 shade A, k6 shade D, k240 shade A, k4 shade D, k2 shade A, k4 shade C, k2 shade A, k58 shade B.

ROWS 24, 25 & 26: Work colours as set on the row above.

ROWS 27 & 28: Using shade A, knit to end.

ROW 29: K40 shade B, k2 shade A, k6 shade C, k2 shade A, k4 shade D, k246 shade A, k6 shade D, k2 shade A, k6 shade C, k2 shade A, k44 shade B.

ROWS 30, 31 & 32: Work colours as set on the row above.

ROWS 33 & 34: Using shade A, knit to end.

ROW 35: K30 shade B, k2 shade A, k8 shade C, k2 shade A, k6 shade D, k256 shade A, k6 shade D, k2 shade A, k10 shade C, k2 shade A, k36 shade B.

ROWS 36, 37 & 38: Work colours as set on the row above.

ROWS 39 & 40: Using shade A, knit to end.

ROW 41: K20 shade B, k2 shade A, k6 shade C, k2 shade A, k6 shade D, k280 shade A, k4 shade D, k2 shade A, k4 shade C, k2 shade A, k32 shade B.

ROWS 42, 43 & 44: Work colours as set on the row above.

Using shade A only, work 4 more rows in garter st.

Cast off loosely.

MAKING UP

※ Sew in any loose ends neatly along a row of sts in the same shade.

TIP: IF YOU WANT TO ADD TASSELS TO THE ENDS OF THE SCARF, MAKE THEM IN RED AND ATTACH TO THE END OF EACH BLOCK OF COLOUR.

SATURN
Mobile

Saturn, named after the Roman god, is the second largest planet in the Solar System. It is orbited by over 50 moons and surrounded by layered rings made up of dust and ice particles. These beautiful rings are perfect for re-creating in a gorgeous multicoloured yarn. When combined with colourful moons, these spherical shapes make a lovely mobile for all ages. Images of Saturn appear in a variety of shades; feel free to choose your own colour palette and add more moons to the mobile if you fancy.

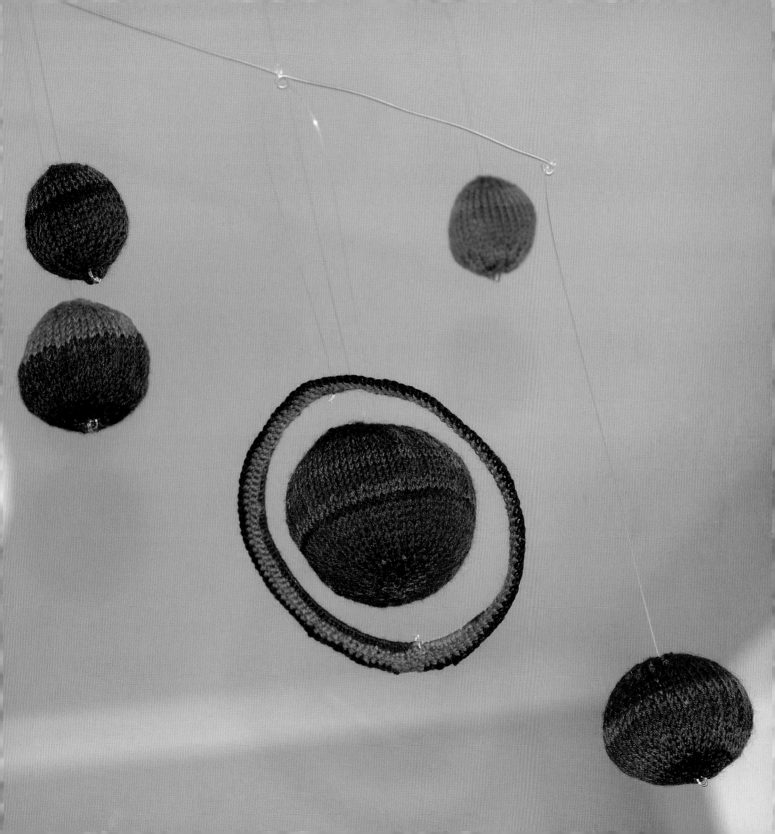

PATTERN *Note*

As Regia Sock yarn is a multicoloured yarn, you can vary the shades of the moons by winding off different batches of colour from one ball of yarn.

SATURN

Cast on 10 sts.

ROW 1 (WS): Purl.

ROW 2: *K1, m1, rep from * to last st, k1. 19 sts.

ROWS 3 & 4: Rep rows 1 & 2. 37 sts.

ROW 5: Purl.

ROW 6: Knit.

ROW 7: Purl.

ROW 8 (RS): *K2, m1, rep from * to last st, k1. 55 sts.

Beg and end with a WS row, work 5 rows in St st.

ROW 14 (RS): *K3, m1, rep from * to last st, k1. 73 sts.

Beg and end with a WS row, work 11 rows in St st.

ROW 26 (RS): *K2, k2tog, rep from * to last st, k1. 55 sts.

Beg and end with a WS row, work 5 rows in St st.

ROW 32 (RS): *K1, k2tog, rep from * to last st, k1. 37 sts.

Beg and end with a WS row, work 3 rows in St st.

ROW 36 (RS): *K2tog, rep from * to last st, k1. 19 sts.

ROW 37: Purl.

ROW 38: Rep row 36. 10 sts rem.

ROW 39: Purl.

Cut yarn, leaving about an 20.5cm (8") tail. Thread tail through rem 10 sts. Keep sts loose; do not pull tail tight yet.

RING

Bend the short length of thinner wire into a circle and join neatly with a piece of sticky tape. Holding the circle of wire, attach the yarn to it and make a sl st on the crochet hook. Hold the yarn at the back of the wire, pass the crochet hook under the wire to loop the yarn through and work a single crochet around the wire. Cont to work a round of SC around the wire making sure that the sts are stretched evenly and cover the wire. Join to the beg of the round with a sl st.

Work 3 more rnds of SC skipping every 4th st on the 3rd round and every 3rd st on the 4th round. Sl the last st with the 1st st of the previous round and fasten off.

LARGE MOON

(Make two)

Cast on 7 sts.

ROW 1 [WS]: Purl.

ROW 2: *K1, m1, rep from * to last st, k1. 13 sts.

ROW 3: Purl.

ROW 4: Rep row 2. 25 sts.

Beg and end with a WS row, work 3 rows in St st.

ROW 8: Rep row 2. 49 sts.

Beg and end with a WS row, work 5 rows in St st.

ROW 14: *K4, m1, rep from * to last 3 sts, k3. 61 sts.

Beg and end with a WS row, work 5 rows in St st.

ROW 20: *K3, k2tog, rep from * to last st, k1. 49 sts.

Beg and end with a WS row. work 5 rows in St st.

ROW 26 [RS]: *K2tog, rep from * to last st, k1. 25 sts.

Beg and end with a purl row, work 3 rows in St st.

ROW 30: Rep row 26. 13 sts.

ROW 31: Purl.

ROW 32: Rep row 26. 7 sts.

ROW 33: Purl.

Cut yarn leaving about an 20.5cm (8") tail. Thread tail through rem 7 sts. Keep sts loose; do not pull tail tight yet.

SMALL MOON

(Make two)

Cast on 5 sts.

ROW 1 (WS): Purl.

ROW 2: *K1, m1, rep from * to last st, k1. 9 sts.

ROW 3: Purl.

ROW 4: Rep row 2. 17 sts.

Beg and end with a WS row, work 3 rows in St st.

ROW 8: Rep row 2. 33 sts.

Beg and end with a WS row, work 11 rows in St st.

ROW 20 (RS): *K2tog, rep from * to last st, k1. 17 sts.

Beg and end with a WS row, work 3 rows in st st.

ROW 24: Rep row 20. 9 sts.

ROW 25: Purl.

ROW 26: Rep row 20. 5 sts.

ROW 27: Purl.

Cut yarn leaving about an 20.5cm (8") tail. Thread tail through rem 10 sts. Keep sts loose; do not pull tail tight yet.

MAKING UP

PLANET AND MOONS

❋ Sew up the side seams and stuff with toy stuffing through the top opening, pull the yarn tight through the sts and fasten off.

MOBILE FRAME

❋ Cut the thicker wire into two lengths measuring about 28cm (11") long, using the pliers make a twist in the centre of each piece and a loop at each end.

❋ Fasten the two pieces of wire to a long length of fishing line, spacing them approx. 25cm (10") apart.

❋ Fasten a length of fishing line to the top of Saturn and suspend from the centre of the bottom piece of wire. Attach a piece of fishing line to opposite sides of the ring, take these two pieces of line up to the centre of the bottom piece of wire, adjusting so that the ring tilts, fasten off.

❋ Attach four separate pieces of line to each of the moons making them different lengths. Attach the two small moons to each end of the top piece of wire and the two large moons to each end of the bottom piece of wire.

TIP: INSTEAD OF USING WIRE FOR THE FRAMEWORK YOU CAN REPLACE THIS WITH FINE PIECES OF WOODEN DOWEL OR RECYCLE OLD WOODEN OR BAMBOO KNITTING NEEDLES.

ATOMIC
Laptop Cover

Atomic theory has been around for thousands of years and while it might still remain a bit of a mystery to most of us, the planetary model shows in simple graphics how electrons spin around a nucleus. The model was created early in the 20th century by a chemist and physicist called Ernest Rutherford and while he probably never imagined it would be used for a knitting pattern, it makes a striking design for this laptop cover. The cover has been felted after knitting to make it more durable and has a simple zip fastening.

MATERIALS

YARN: Aran weight.

Shown here: Rowan Creative Focus Worsted (75% wool, 25% alpaca; 220m (200yd)/100g): ebony (A), 2 balls; saffron (B) and natural (C), 1 ball each.

NEEDLES: Sizes 4 and 4.5mm: straight.

Adjust needle size if necessary to obtain the correct tension.

HABERDASHERY: 38cm (15") black zip; tracing paper; tapestry needle; pins; sewing needle and matching thread.

TENSION: 20 sts and 24 rows to 10cm (4") measured in St st using larger needles.

20 sts and 20 rows to 8.5cm (3¼") after washing.

FINISHED MEASUREMENTS: (after washing) 28cm (11") tall x 38cm (15") wide.

SCORE: 50 POINTS

PATTERN *Note*

The cover is knitted in one piece starting at the top edge of the back, the atoms are knitted on the front using the intarsia method (see page 14) and the rings are embroidered in chain stitch (see page 16) after the cover has been washed.

BACK AND FRONT

Using shade A and smaller needles, cast on 96 sts.

Knit 2 rows.

Change to larger needles and beg and end with a RS row work 75 rows in St st.

NEXT ROW [WS]: Knit.

Work 16 rows in St st, ending with a WS row.

Establish chart as foll, reading from right to left on RS rows and from left to right on WS rows.

NEXT ROW [RS]: K29 with A, beg with 1st st of row 1 of chart, work all 38 sts of chart changing colour where indicated, k29 with A.

NEXT ROW: P29 with A, work row 2 of chart reading from left to right, p29 with A.

Rep the last 2 rows until all 39 rows of chart have been worked, ending with a RS row.

Cont working in St st in shade A only until 75 rows have been worked from the turning row, ending with a WS row.

Change to smaller needles, knit 2 rows.

CO all sts kwise.

Atomic Laptop Cover

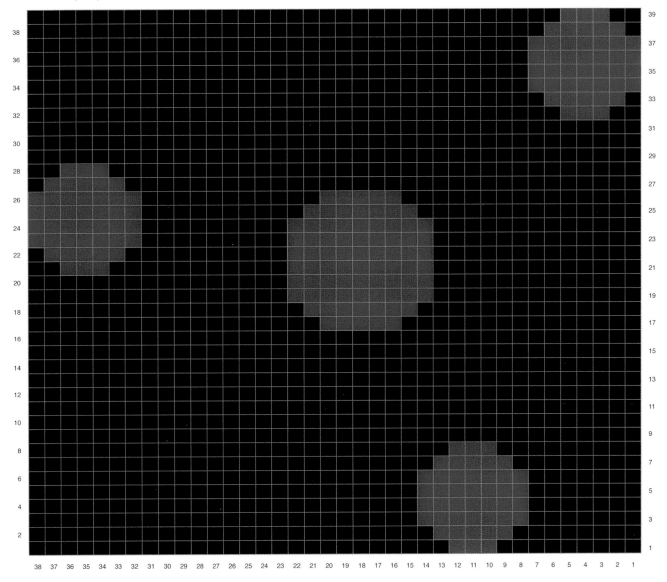

KEY
- ■ A
- ■ B

MAKING UP

* Fold the case in half along the turning row and sew up the two short side seams.

* Machine wash at 122°F (50°C). Gently stretch into shape while damp and pin out on a board ensuring that all the edges are square.

When it is dry, work the chain st as foll:

* Draw an oval-shaped template on to a piece of tracing paper and cut out. Pin the oval shape vertically onto the front of the work ensuring that the larger sphere is centred in the middle and the bottom sphere is centred on the lower right hand edge of the oval. Using shade C, work in chain st around the entire shape.

* Remove the template and place diagonally across the work, ensuring the large sphere is centred in the middle and the smaller sphere to the left is centred on the top left hand edge of the oval. Pin the template in place and chain st all the way round as before.

* Remove the template and place diagonally across the work, ensuring the large sphere is centred in the middle and the smaller sphere at the top right is centred on the top edge of the oval. Pin the template in place and chain st all the way round as before.

* Make a circular template from a plate (this should measure about 20.5cm (8") in diameter) that is slightly larger than the design already stitched; pin the template over the design and chain st a sphere around the entire design.

* Sew the zip into the opening.

TIP: IF SUBSTITUTING THE YARN WITH A DIFFERENT BRAND, MAKE SURE IT IS PURE WOOL OR A WOOL AND ALPACA BLEND WITH INSTRUCTIONS FOR HAND WASHING. THIS WILL BE SUITABLE TO ACHIEVE THE FELTED EFFECT. REMEMBER, WHEN FELTING IT IS ALWAYS BETTER TO WASH AT A COOLER TEMPERATURE FIRST, THEN IF NECESSARY YOU CAN WASH AGAIN AT A HIGHER TEMPERATURE FOR FURTHER SHRINKAGE.

SPACE ROCKET
Desk Tidy

The inspiration for these retro designs came from vintage comic strips depicting colourful rockets shooting through space. Transformed into useful pots the rockets will keep your work space tidy, providing storage for pens and pencils in the short version and knitting needles, rulers, and paint brushes in the taller one. They also make the perfect gift for all ages; fill them with candy and enjoy. You can adjust the colours to suit your décor, or use up yarn oddments and knit them in multicoloured stripes.

MATERIALS

YARN: Aran weight.

Shown here: Rowan Handknit Cotton (100% cotton; 93m (85yd)/50g):

Short Rocket: sea foam (A), Florence (orange) (B) and black (C), 1 ball each.

Tall Rocket: rosso (red) (A) 2 balls; ecru (B) and black (C), 1 ball each.

NEEDLES: 3.25 and 6mm: straight; 4mm: double pointed needles.

HABERDASHERY: Removable stitch markers (m), 3.5mm crochet hook, toy stuffing, 12.5cm (5") tall x 32cm (12½") circumference glass jar, 23cm (9") circumference cardboard tube, tapestry needle.

TENSION: 20 sts and 26 rows to 10cm (4") in St st using larger needles.

- - - - - - - - - - - - - - - - - -

FINISHED MEASUREMENT:

SHORT ROCKET – about 17.5cm in length x 27cm in circumference (before stretching).

TALL ROCKET – about 27.5cm length x 25cm in circumference (before stretching).

PATTERN *Note*

If you want to make either rocket larger or smaller, add or subtract 4 sts to the total amount cast on. Each block of 4 sts will increase or decrease the circumference by just under 2.5cm (1").

SHORT ROCKET

MAIN BODY

Using larger dpns and shade A, cast on 48 sts.

Work in the round as foll:

K2, p2 rib for 4 rnds.

Work in St st for 4 rnds.

If the jar you have chosen is straight, continue in St st without shaping until the sleeve reaches the top of the jar.

If the jar is shaped as shown in the image, cont as foll:

NEXT ROUND: M1, k24, m1, k24. 50 sts.

Work 4 rnds in St st.

NEXT ROUND: M1, k25, m1, k25. 52 sts.

Work 10 rnds in St st.

NEXT ROUND: K2tog, k24, k2tog, k24. 50 sts.

Change to yarn B.

Work 4 rnds in St st.

NEXT ROUND: K2tog, k23, k2tog, k23. 48 sts.

Work 10 rnds in St st.

NEXT ROUND: *K2 with A, p2 with B; rep from * to end of round.

Rep last round 7 more times.

Cast off.

SIDE JETS

(Make 3)

With RS of the rocket body facing, space 3 removable markers into fabric evenly around the cast-on edge of bottom rib. Using a crochet hook and yarn A, beg at the first marker, pull a loop under the bar between each st for 22 rows up the side of the rocket until there are 22 sts on the crochet

SCORE: 25 POINTS

hook. Place these sts on a smaller needle so that the tip of the needle is facing the top of the rocket.

Using shade B, continue as foll:

ROW 1: Knit.

ROW 2: K18, w&t, knit back to beg of row.

ROW 4: K14, w&t back to beg of row.

ROW 6: K10, w&t back to beg of row.

ROW 8: K6, w&t back to beg of row.

ROW 10: K2, w&t back to beg of row.

Cast off all 22 sts.

Rep at the remaining 2 markers.

MAKING UP

✳ Sew in any loose ends.

PORTHOLES
(Make 2)

Using shade C and crochet hook, ch6, form into ring with sl st into 1st ch.

ROUND 1: Ch 1, work 11 sc into centre of ring, join round with sl st into 1st sc. 11 sc.

ROUND 2: Ch 1, sc into 1st st, work 2sc into every st to end of round, join round with sl st into 1st sc. 21 sc.

ROUND 3: Using shade B, ch1, *2sc into next st, sc into next st; rep from * to end of round. Join round with sl st into 1st sc. 28 sc.

FASTEN OFF
Sew the two portholes onto the front of the rocket body as shown in the image.

TALL ROCKET

MAIN BODY

Using shade A and larger needles, cast on 50 sts.

ROW 1 [RS]: *K2 with A, p2 with B; rep from * to last 2 sts, k2 shade A.

ROW 2: *P2 with A, k2 with B; rep rom * to last 2 sts, p2 shade A.

Rep last 2 rows 2 more times.

Beg and end with a RS row and using shade A, work 11 rows in St st.

NEXT ROW [WS]: Using shade B knit to end of row.

NEXT ROW [RS]: K13 shade A, k12 shade B, k12 shade A, k13 shade B.

NEXT ROW: P13 shade B, p12 shade A, p12 shade B, p13 shade A.

Rep last 2 rows 6 more times.

NEXT ROW: K13 shade B, k12 shade A, k12 shade B, k13 shade A.

NEXT ROW: P13 shade A, p12 shade B, p12 shade A, p13 shade B.

Rep last 2 rows 6 more times.

NEXT ROW [RS]: Using shade B purl to end.

Beg and end with a WS row, and using A, work 15 rows in St st.

NEXT ROW: *K2 shade A, p2 shade B; rep from * to last 2 sts, k2 shade A.

NEXT ROW: *P2 shade A, k2 shade B, rep from * to last 2 sts, p2 shade A.

Rep last 2 rows 4 more times.

CO all sts using shade A.

SIDE JETS

(Make 4)

Worked from top edge downward. Using shade A and smaller needles, cast on 20 sts.

Beg with a RS row work 8 rows in St st, ending with a WS row.

NEXT ROW: Cast off 4, k to end of row. 16 sts rem.

NEXT ROW: Cast off 4, purl to end of row. 12 sts rem.

Beg with a RS row work 16 rows in St st, ending with a WS row.

NEXT ROW: K2tog to end. 6 sts rem.

Thread yarn through rem sts and leave open for stuffing.

TIP: YOU CAN USE GLASS JARS OR CARDBOARD TUBES FOR THE CONTAINER AND ADJUST THE LENGTH OF THE ROCKET TO SUIT YOUR CHOSEN CONTAINER. I HAVE USED A CURVED GLASS JAR FOR THE SHORT ROCKET AND CUT THE TOP THIRD OFF A CARDBOARD WHISKY CONTAINER FOR THE TALL ROCKET.

MAKING UP

❋ With RS together and using mattress stitch sew up the seam on the main body of the rocket.

❋ Sew up the seams on each of the side jets, from cast on edge up to last row. Stuff firmly with toy stuffing, pull the yarn tight through the stitches and fasten off.

❋ Fasten each jet to the rocket body spacing them evenly as shown in the image.

PORTHOLES
(Make 3)

Using shade C and crochet hook, ch6, join into a ring with sl st into 1st ch.

ROUND 1: Ch1, work 11 sc into centre of ring, join into a ring with sl st into 1st sc. 11 sc.

ROUND 2: Ch1, 1sc into 1st st, work 2sc into every st to end of round, join round with sl st into 1sc. 21 sc.

ROUND 3: Using shade B, ch1, *2sc into next st, sc into next st; rep from * to end of round, join round with sl st into 1st sc. 28 sc.

FASTEN OFF

Sew the three portholes onto the front of the rocket body as shown in the image.

FLYING SAUCER
Paperweight

The Flying Saucer is an icon of the fifties and has appeared in many comic strips and sci-fi movies. The metallic yarn gives this scaled-down model a space-age sparkle. Use dried beans to stuff the main body and it will make a great paperweight for the office; alternatively make a lighter version for the kids by just using toy stuffing. The main body is knitted in two pieces using the short-row shaping technique and then joined with a three-needle cast off to create a neat ridge around the edge.

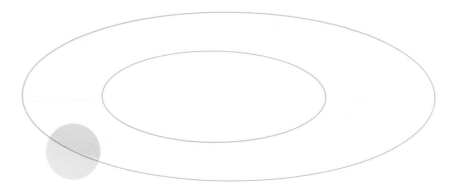

MATERIALS

YARN: DK weight.

Shown here: Rowan Cotton Glacé (100% cotton; 126m (115yd)/50g): ecru (A), dawn grey (B), 1 ball each.

4-ply.

Shown here: Rowan Shimmer (60% cupro, 40% polyester; 191m (175yd)/25g): silver (C), 1 ball.

NEEDLES: 2.75mm and 3.25mm: straight; two 40cm circular needles.

Adjust needle size if necessary to obtain the correct tension.

HABERDASHERY: Stitch marker (m), 2 plastic card or polystyrene saucers (about 16.5cm (6½") in diameter), 10 small black press studs, toy stuffing, dried beans, sticky tape, matching sewing thread and needle, tapestry needle.

TENSION: 23 sts and 32 rows to 10cm (4") using 3.25mm needles over St st.

FINISHED MEASUREMENTS: Approx. 17.5cm in diameter x 9cm high.

SCORE: 20 POINTS

PATTERN Note

The saucer shape is knitted in two pieces using the short-row shaping technique (see page 15); the dome of the cabin is stuffed with toy stuffing and sewn on afterwards, then the top and bottom are joined together with a three-needle cast off.

SAUCER BASE

Using shade A, and smaller needles cast on 20 sts.

ROW 1: Knit.

ROW 2: Purl.

Cont working short-row shaping as foll:

ROWS 3 & 4: K18, turn, sl1, purl to end.

ROWS 5 & 6: K16, turn, sl1, purl to end.

ROWS 7 & 8: K14, turn, sl1, purl to end.

ROWS 9 & 10: K12, turn, sl1, purl to end.

ROWS 11 & 12: K10, turn, sl1, purl to end.

ROWS 13 & 14: K8, turn, sl1, purl to end.

ROWS 15 & 16: K6, turn, sl1, purl to end.

ROWS 17 & 18: K4, turn, sl1 pwise wyf, purl to end

Rep the last 18 rows more times

Rep Rows 1 and 2 once more.

Cast off.

Neatly sew together the cast on and cast off edges.

With RS of work facing and using larger circular needle and a strand each of yarns B and yarn C held together, pick up and knit 120 sts around outer edge of base. Pm for beg of rnd.

Working in the round in St st, continue for 6 rnds. Leave these sts on the circular needle, cut yarn.

Thread a tapestry needle with yarn A and using running st gather the opening at the centre of the base, pull tight and fasten off.

SAUCER TOP

Work as for saucer base, leaving the 120 sts on the second circular needle, but with the centre hole open.

CABIN DOME

Using larger needles and one strand each of yarns B and C held together, cast on 49 sts.

Knit 4 rows.

Beg with a RS row, cont in St st for 4 rows, ending with a WS row.

ROW 1: *K5, k2tog, rep from * to end of row. 42 sts.

Next and every WS row: Purl.

ROW 3: *K4, k2tog, rep from * to end of row. 35 sts.

ROW 5: *K3, k2tog, rep from * to end of row. 28 sts.

ROW 7: *K2, k2tog, rep from * to end of row. 21 sts.

ROW 9: *K1, k2tog, rep from * to end of row. 14 sts.

ROW 10: P2tog to end of row. 7 sts.

ROW 11: K2tog (3 times), k1. 4 sts rem.

Break yarn and thread through rem sts, pull tight.

MAKING UP

❋ Stitch the side seam of the cabin dome. Place the dome over the centre hole of the top of the saucer and stitch neatly in place making sure it is central. Fill the dome of the cabin with toy stuffing through the hole in the saucer top until it is firm.

❋ Fill one of the plastic saucers with the dried beans and pad out with toy stuffing so that it fills the second plastic saucer when it is placed on top face down. Ensure that the stuffing fills the two saucers so that they don't get dented. Join the two saucers together with sticky tape.

❋ Place the knitted saucer top and base with WS together, holding the needle tips together from each piece in the left hand and,

using a smaller needle and yarn B only, *ktog the two 1st sts from each needle*. Rep with the next two sts from each needle, so that there are two sts on the RH needle. Cast off the first st. Rep from * to * casting off as you go until you are just over half way around the saucer. Now place the plastic saucers inside the knitted pieces and continue to cast off as before.

❋ With sewing thread and needle, stitch one half of the press studs around the base of the cabin spacing them evenly along the garter st border.

TIP: IF YOU DON'T WANT TO USE THIS AS A PAPERWEIGHT IT CAN BE FILLED WITH JUST TOY STUFFING. FOLLOW THE INSTRUCTIONS THROUGHOUT, BUT INSTEAD OF USING THE PLASTIC SAUCERS WORK THE RIDGE CAST OFF UNTIL THERE IS JUST A SMALL OPENING, FILL WITH TOY STUFFING UNTIL IT IS FIRM AND CAST OFF THE REMAINING STITCHES.

SPACE-RACE
Mobile

Space rockets are a classic symbol used to decorate a child's bedroom and have massive appeal. These brightly coloured rockets are easy to knit in simple stocking stitch with garter stitch ridges and the colour combinations can be varied. This is a great project for using up your yarn stash, as only small amounts are needed for each rocket and if you stick to a fine or medium weight yarn the rockets will not get too large.

MATERIALS

YARN: DK weight.

Shown here: Rowan Cotton Glacé (100% cotton; 126m (115yd)/50g): persimmon (orange) (A), nightshade (navy) (B), bubbles (pink) (C), shoot (green) (D), poppy (red) (E), oyster (F), 1 ball each.

NEEDLES: 2.75mm: straight.

Adjust needle size if necessary to obtain the correct tension.

HABERDASHERY: Toy stuffing 56cm (22") of fine wire (about 1.5mm width), about 150cm (60") fishing line (.70mm), pair of blunt-nosed pliers, pair of wire cutters, piece of black felt fabric measuring about 5cm (2") x 35.5cm (14"), scissors, sewing needle and gold metallic embroidery thread, tapestry needle.

TENSION: 24 sts and 34 rows to 10cm (4").

FINISHED MEASUREMENT: 12.5cm (5") to 15cm (6").

SCORE: 20 POINTS

PATTERN Note

Make sure that your tension is tight and even so that the stuffing doesn't show through the knitting. For small items like this, you can also use leftover yarn oddments for stuffing.

ROCKET 1

Using shade A, cast on 4 sts.

ROW 1 (RS): Knit.

ROW 2: Purl.

ROW 3: *K1, m1, rep from * to last st, k1. 7 sts.

ROW 4: Purl.

Rep last 2 rows once. 13 sts.

Beg with a RS row, work 4 rows in St st.

ROW 11: Rep row 3. 25 sts.

ROWS 12 & 13: K using shade B.

ROWS 14 & 15: K using shade A.

ROWS 16 & 17: Rep rows 13 & 14.

Beg with a WS row, work 24 rows in St st using shade B.

Using shade A for remainder, cont as foll:

Knit 2 rows.

Purl 1 row.

NEXT ROW: K2tog to last st, k1. 13 sts.

Purl 1 row.

Rep last 2 rows twice. 4 sts.

Thread yarn through rem sts.

FINS
(Make 3)

Using shade A, cast on 3 sts.

Purl 1 WS row.

NEXT ROW: K1, m1, k1, m1, k1. 5 sts.

Purl 1 row.

NEXT ROW: K2, m1, k1, m1, k2. 7 sts.

Purl 1 row.

NEXT ROW: K3, m1, k1, m1, k3. 9 sts.

Purl 1 row.

NEXT ROW: K4, m1, k1, m1, k4. 11 sts.

Beg and end with a p row, work 5 rows in St st.

NEXT ROW: k3, skp, k1, k2tog, k3. 9 sts.

Purl 1 row.

NEXT ROW: K2, skp, k1, k2tog, k2. 5 sts.

Purl 1 row.

NEXT ROW: K1, skp, k1, k2tog, k1. 5 sts.

Thread yarn through rem 5 sts.

ROCKET 2

Using shade C, cast on 4 sts.

ROW 1 [RS]: Knit.

ROW 2: Purl.

ROW 3: *K1, m1, rep from * to last st, k1. 7 sts.

ROW 4: Purl.

Rep last 2 rows once. 13 sts.

ROW 7: Knit.

ROW 8: Knit.

Beg with a k row work 4 rows in St st.

ROW 13: *K1, m1, rep from * to last st, k1. 25 sts.

ROW 14: Knit.

Beg with a RS row, cont in St st working the foll stripe sequence.

2 rows B.

2 rows D.

2 rows C.

Rep the last 6 rows 3 more times.

Knit 2 rows in B.

Using shade C for remainder, cont as foll:

Beg with a RS row work 4 rows in St st.

NEXT ROW [RS]: K2tog to last st, k1. 13 sts.

NEXT ROW: Purl.

Rep last 2 rows twice. 4 sts.

Thread yarn through rem sts.

FINS
(Make 3)

Using shade C, work same as the Fins for Rocket 1.

ROCKET 3

Using shade E, cast on 14 sts.

ROW 1 (RS): *K2 shade E, p2 shade F; rep from * to last 2 sts, k2 shade E.

ROW 2: P2 shade E, k2 shade F; rep from * to last 2 sts, p2 shade E.

Rep Rows 1 and 2 twice more, then row 1 once more.

Using shade E only, cont as foll:

ROW 8 (WS): Purl to end.

ROW 9: *K1, m1; rep from * to last st, k1. 27 sts.

Beg and end with a WS row, work 7 rows in St st.

ROW 17: *K4, m1; rep from * to last 3 sts, k3. 33 sts.

ROW 18: Knit using shade F.

Beg and end with a RS row and using shade F, work 13 rows in St st.

Change to shade E and cont as foll:

ROW 32 (WS): Knit.

ROW 33: *K4, k2tog; rep from * to last 3 sts, k3. 28 sts.

Beg and end with a WS row, work 2 rows in St st.

Rep last 2 rows using shade F.

Purl 1 row using shade E.

ROW 39: Using shade E, k2tog to end of row. 14 sts.

Rep last 2 rows using shade F, then once again using shade E.

Thread yarn through rem sts.

FINS

(Make 3)

Using shade E, work same as the Fins for Rocket 1.

ROCKET 4

Work same as for Rocket 3, using the foll shades:

A instead of E.

D instead of F.

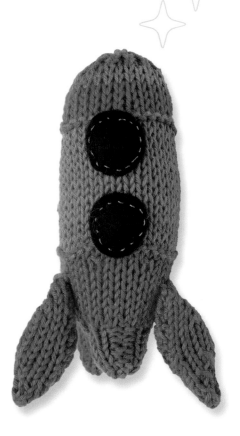

MAKING UP

* Sew up the seam on each rocket leaving the tip open. Stuff firmly through the opening, pull the stitches tight at the tip and fasten off. Sew the seam on the fins, leaving a small opening, stuff firmly, sew up the opening and neatly attach the fins to the main body.

PORTHOLES

* Cut eight small discs from the felt fabric, each measuring approx. 4.5cm (1¾") in diameter (you can draw round a coin of similar measurements). Sew two portholes onto the front of each rocket using the metallic thread and working in running stitch.

FRAME

* Cut the wire into two lengths measuring about 28cm (11"); using the pliers make a twist in the centre of each piece and a loop at each end.

* Fasten the two pieces of wire to a long length of fishing line, spacing them about 25.5cm (10") apart.

* Fasten a length of fishing line to the top third of each rocket body, so that it hangs at an angle and attach the other end of the line to the wire frames, adjusting the lengths so that the rockets hang at different heights.

TIP: INSTEAD OF MAKING A MOBILE, THESE MAKE GREAT LITTLE TOY POCKET ROCKETS FOR KIDS.

ROBO
Dog Coat

Robotic dogs appear in all shapes and sizes, but however well-behaved, clean, quiet and obedient they are you can't beat the real thing. This cute coat will keep your pooch toasty on chilly days – knitted in machine washable pure wool it is warm and practical. The simple robotic dog design is knitted using the Fair Isle method and is a good introduction to colour work for less experienced knitters. The pattern instructions are designed for a small dog but could easily adjusted for larger models (see the tip box for how to increase the size of the coat).

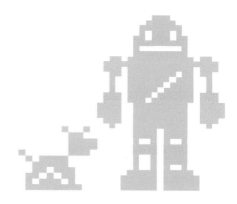

MATERIALS

YARN: DK weight.

Shown here: Rowan Pure Wool DK (100% superwash wool; 137m (125yd)/50g): pier (A), black (B) and dahlia, 1 ball each.

NEEDLES: Coat – 4mm: straight; Chest Straps – 3.25mm: straight.

Adjust needle size if necessary to obtain the correct tension.

HABERDASHERY: Stitch holder; row counter; 5 x small buttons; removable stitch markers (m); tapestry needle.

TENSION: 25 sts and 27 rows to 10cm (4") in Fair Isle pattern using larger needles.

FINISHED MEASUREMENT: 30cm (12") long from base to neck x 16.5cm (6½") wide across back (about 40cm (16") around widest part of chest).

SCORE: 50 POINTS

PATTERN *Note*

The design is worked in St st using the Fair Isle method. Read the chart from right to left on the RS rows and from left to right on the WS rows.

COAT

Using shade A and larger needles, cast on 41 sts.

ROWS 1 & 2: Knit.

ROW 3 (RS): Knit.

ROW 4: K2, purl to last 2 sts, k2.

ROW 5: K2 with A, beg at the first st of Row 1 of chart, work the 12 st pattern rep to the last 3 sts, work st 13 of chart, k2 shade A.

ROW 6: K2 shade A, p st 13 of Row 2 of chart, work the 12 st pattern rep to the last 2 sts, k2 shade A.

The last 2 rows establish the pattern. Cont until 60 rows have been worked from cast on edge, placing a marker at both ends of Rows 30 and 50.

SIDE SHAPING

ROW 61 (RS): K2, m1, cont with 12 st pattern rep as est to last 2 sts, m1, k2. 43 sts.

Work 9 rows even as est.

ROW 71: Rep Row 61. 45 sts.

Work 8 rows even as est, ending with a RS row.

NECK SHAPING

Cont as foll using A only:

ROW 80 (WS): Knit.

ROW 81: K2, m1, k13, place rem sts on a st holder. 16 sts rem.

RIGHT NECK STRAP

Working on these 16 sts only, cont in garter st, working the foll shapings:

ROW 82 (WS): K2tog, knit to end. 15 sts.

ROW 83: Knit to last 2 sts, k2tog. 14 sts.

ROW 84: Rep Row 82. 13 sts.

Beg and end with a RS row, work 3 rows in St st.

ROW 88 (WS): Rep Row 82. 12 sts.

Beg with a RS row, work 2 rows in St st.

Cont straight until neck strap measures 8.5cm (3¼") from beg of neck shaping, ending with WS row.

BUTTONHOLE ROW: K2, yo, k2tog, k4, yo, k2tog, k2.

Knit 3 rows. Cast off.

Return 30 held sts to needle and rejoin yarn with RS facing. Cont in garter st as foll:

ROW 81 [RS]: Cast off centre 15 sts, knit to last 2 sts, m1, k2. 16 sts.

LEFT NECK STRAP

Working on these 16 sts only, cont in garter st, working the foll shapings:

ROW 82 [WS]: Knit to last 2 sts, skp. 15 sts.

ROW 83: Skp, knit to end. 14 sts.

ROW 84: Rep Row 82. 13 sts.

Beg and end with a RS row, work 3 rows in St st.

ROW 88 [WS]: Rep Row 82. 12 sts.

Beg with a RS row, work 2 rows in St st.

ROW 91 [RS]: K2, m1, knit to end. 13 sts.

ROW 92: Rep Row 82. 12 sts.

Cont straight until neck strap meas 10cm (4") from beg of neck shaping, ending with a WS row.

Robo Dog Coat

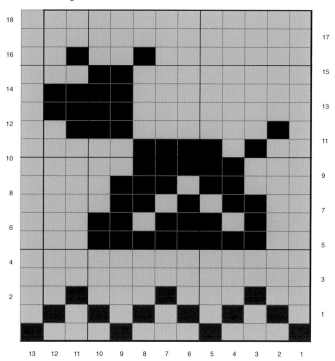

KEY

- ▨ A
- ■ B
- ■ C

PATTERN REPEAT

TIP: TO ENLARGE FOR A MEDIUM-SIZED DOG, CAST ON 12 EXTRA STS AND WORK 1 EXTRA PATTERN REPEATED ACROSS THE WIDTH AND LENGTH OF THE COAT, CAST OFF THE 12 STS WITH THE 15 STS FOR THE NECK.

MAKING UP

❋ Sew in loose ends, block to measurements.

RIGHT CHEST STRAP

❋ With RS of work facing, using shade A and smaller needles, pick up and knit 20 sts between the two markers on the right-hand edge of work.

❋ Work in garter st for 8.5cm (3¼"), ending with a WS row.

❋ Buttonhole row: K2, [yo, k2tog, k5] twice, yo, k2tog, k2.

❋ Knit 3 rows.

❋ Cast off.

LEFT CHEST STRAP

❋ Work as for right chest strap, between the two markers on the left hand side of work, but omit the buttonholes. Cont until work measures 10cm (4"), ending with a WS row.

❋ Cast off.

❋ Sew the buttons onto left neck strap and left chest strap to correspond with the buttonholes.

CASSETTE MUSIC
Player Cover

The audio cassette is a blast from the past. When they first appeared, these neat little tapes were space-age technology compared to the large and bulky reel-to-reel tapes. The compact plastic covers came in a variety of colours and survived for a couple of decades before being supplanted by CDs. The graphic lines and bright colours of the retro cassette make a handy little cover for a modern-day music player. The design is knitted using both the intarsia and Fair Isle methods and can be lined with felt fabric to provide a tidy finish.

MATERIALS

YARN: DK weight.

Shown here: Rowan Cotton Glacé (100% cotton; 126m (115yd)/50g): nightshade (navy) (A), bubbles (pink) (B) and ecru (C), 1 ball each.

NEEDLES: 3.25mm: straight.

Adjust needle size if necessary to obtain the correct tension.

HABERDASHERY: 1 x piece of felt measuring 13.5cm (5¼") x 18cm (7"), 1 small press stud, scissors, sewing needle and thread, tapestry needle.

TENSION: 26 sts and 34 rows to 10cm (4") in pattern

FINISHED MEASUREMENTS:
About 13.5cm (5¼") x 9cm (3½")

SCORE: 40 POINTS

PATTERN *Note*

The design is knitted sideways starting at the middle of the back.

COVER

Using shade A, cast on 35 sts.

ROW 1 [RS]: K1, p1, knit to end.

ROW 2: Purl to last 3 sts, k1, p1, k1.

Rep these 2 rows 6 more times.

ROW 15: Rep Row 1.

TURNING ROW [WS]: Knit to end.

FRONT

ROW 17 [RS]: Reading chart from right to left on RS rows and left to right on WS rows, beg at Row 1 of chart and cont in St st changing colours as indicated. AT THE SAME TIME cont to work the first 3 sts of every RS row and last 3 sts of every WS row in moss st as est.

When row 29 of chart has been completed cont as foll:

TURNING ROW [WS]: Using shade A, knit to end.

Rep Rows 1–15.

Cast off purlwise.

MAKING UP

❊ Sew in loose ends, block and press carefully.

❊ Fold cover at turning rows and use the mattress St to sew centre back seam (cast on and cast off edges). Straighten out so that the seam runs down the centre of the back and stitch the seam along the base of the cover, leaving the moss stitch end open.

LINING

❊ Fold the piece of felt in half so that it measures 13.5 x 9cm (5¼ x 3½"); trim if necessary so that it will fit snugly inside the cover. With sewing needle and thread, stitch down the long edge and along the bottom seam. Place inside the knitted cover and neatly stitch in place along the inside of the top edge.

❊ Fasten the press stud to the inside of the moss stitch edging.

Cassette Cover

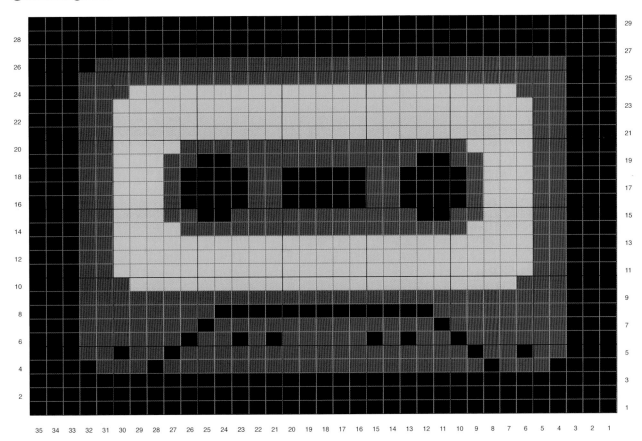

KEY

■ A

■ B

■ C

TIP: IF PREFERRED, THE SMALL AREAS OF PATTERN ON THE CHART CAN BE WORKED BY SWISS DARNING INSTEAD OF FAIR ISLE. DO THIS BEFORE STITCHING THE SEAMS.

ROBOT
Pot Holders

Toy robots have been collectors' items for decades; they have a classic appeal with a touch of humour. Their angular lines and bright colours create the perfect image for a knitting design. These three chaps make a funky set of pot holders to liven up your kitchen. They are knitted in soft cotton for easy care and the double-knit method provides a thick layer to protect your hands from burning.

MATERIALS

YARN: Aran weight.

Shown here: Rowan Handknit Cotton (100% cotton; 93m (85yd)/50g): linen (A), 3 balls; pacific (purple) (B), rosso (red) (C) and atlantic (teal) (D), 1 ball each.

NEEDLES: 4mm: straight.
HABERDASHERY: 3.5mm crochet hook, tapestry needle.

TENSION: 20 sts and 28 rows to 10cm (4") in St st.

- - - - - - - - - - - - - - - - -

FINISHED MEASUREMENTS:
About 18cm (7") square.

SCORE: 70 POINTS

PATTERN *Note*

The double-knit method creates a two-sided fabric. The first figure given is the st count in shade A and the figure in brackets is the total number of sts in shades A and B. When working with two colours, it is important to keep the colour sequence correct. The pattern from the chart will appear on the reverse side of the knitting in the opposite colours, i.e. the robot will appear in shade A and the background will be the contrast shade.

POT HOLDER 1

Cast on 35 sts with a strand of shade A and a strand of shade B held together to make a total of (70) sts. Ensure that the 2 colours alternate (A, B) all the way along the cast on row.

ROW 1: K1 A, *bring both strands of yarn to the front of work and p1 B, take both strands of yarn to the back of work and k1 A; rep from * to the last st, p1 B.

ROW 2: K1 B, *bring both strands of yarn to the front of work and p1 A , take both strands of yarn to the back of work and k1 B; rep from * to the last st, p1 A.

Rep these rows 2 more times.

Est chart as foll:

ROW 7: K1 A, *bring both strands of yarn to the front of work and p1 B, take both strands of yarn to the back of work and k1 A; rep from * 4 more times, p1 B,

TIP: IF DOUBLE KNITTING SOUNDS ALL TOO COMPLICATED, WORK TWO SEPARATE PIECES FOR EACH POT HOLDER IN ST ST THROUGHOUT. CAST ON 35 STS AND, WORKING 6 ROWS BEFORE AND AFTER THE CHART AND 6 STS EITHER SIDE OF IT. COMPLETE AS NORMAL. WORK THE SECOND PIECE IN THE SAME WAY, REVERSING THE COLOURS. PLACE THE TWO PIECES WS TOGETHER, STITCH NEATLY AROUND EACH EDGE AND THEN WORK THE DOUBLE CROCHET EDGING AND LOOP. ALTERNATIVELY, KNIT JUST ONE PIECE AND BACK WITH A PIECE OF FABRIC.

Pot Holder 1

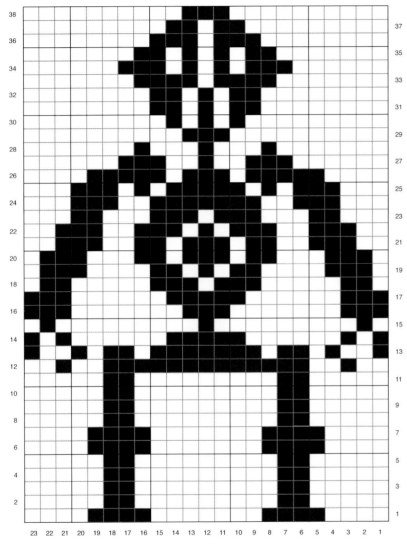

KEY

☐ A

■ B

(12 sts worked). Keeping the double knit method correct and reading the chart from right to left on the odd numbered (RS) rows and from left to right on the even numbered (WS) rows work the 23 (46) sts from the chart working the knit sts in the shade indicated on the chart and the purl sts in the second shade. When the 23 (46) sts of the chart have been completed work the last 6 (12) sts as est.

ROW 8: Work the first 6 (12) sts as est, then work Row 2 of the chart. Change colours as indicated in the chart (remembering that the contrast shade will appear as the main shade on all even numbered rows), complete the 23 (46) sts of chart pattern and work to the end of row as est.

These 2 rows establish the chart.

Note: Take care not to twist the 2 strands of yarn.

Work all 38 rows of the chart, then continue as foll:

Rep Rows 1 and 2 three times.

Pot Holder 2

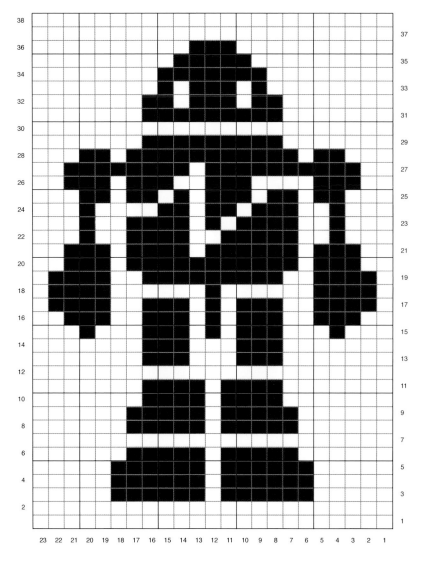

KEY

□ A

■ C

MAKING UP

❋ Sew in any loose ends. Using shade A or the contrast shade and the crochet hook, beg at the top left hand corner, work in single crochet all the way around the pot holder, working 4SC into the st at each corner. When you are back at the first corner work a chain of 14 sts, loop this in half and fasten at the corner with a sl st.

POT HOLDER 2

Work as for Pot Holder 1 using shade A and shade C.

POT HOLDER 3

Work as for Pot Holder 1, using shade A and shade D and placing chart 4 (8) sts in from edge instead of 6 (12) sts.

Pot Holder 3

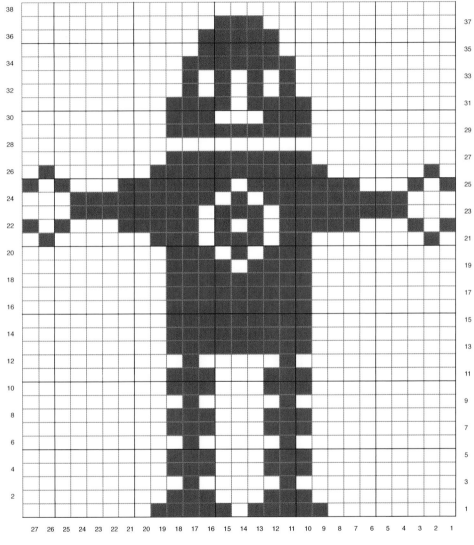

KEY

☐ A

■ D

CIRCUIT BOARD
Beanie & Fingerless Mitts

Circuit boards look a bit like a maze, with hundreds of circuits printed onto a surface forming fantastic geometric designs, sometimes in vibrant blues and greens. The circuit pattern creates a natural design for knitting and makes a relatively easy to follow Fair Isle pattern, working with just two shades. Keep your favourite techie warm with a beanie and mitts. For the perfect gift set, knit the matching scarf as well.

MATERIALS

YARN: Aran weight .

Shown here: Debbie Bliss Cashmerino Aran (55% merino wool, 33% microfibre, 12% cashmere; 90m (98yd)/50g): kahki (A), 3 balls; lime green (B), 1 ball.

(Note: The yarn quantities stated are sufficient to knit the beanie and mitts.)

NEEDLES: 4.5 and 5mm: straight. Adjust needle size if necessary to obtain the correct tension.

HABERDASHERY: 29 x small buttons, tapestry needle.

TENSION: 19 sts and 24 rows to 10cm (4") in pattern using larger needles.

- - - - - - - - - - - - - - - - - -

FINISHED MEASUREMENTS:

MITTS – about 19.5cm (7¾") total length x 25cm (9¾") around hand.

BEANIE – about 24cm (9½") total length x 48.5cm (19") in circumference (will stretch to fit a head measuring up to 61cm (24")).

SCORE: 55 POINTS

PATTERN Note

Knit using the Fair Isle method, weaving the yarn at the back of the work across 2 or 3 sts. The button embellishments are sewn on after knitting.

BEANIE

Using larger needles and A, cast on 90 sts.

ROW 1 (RS): *K2, p2; rep from * to last 2 sts, k2.

ROW 2: *P2, k2; rep from * to last 2 sts, k2.

Rep Rows 1 and 2 six more times.

Beg with a RS row, work in St st throughout as foll:

NEXT ROW: Beg at Row 1 of Beanie chart, work the 30 stitch pattern rep, changing colours as indicated.

Cont until all 30 rows of chart have been completed.

CROWN SHAPING

ROW 1: Using shade A only [k2tog, k7] 10 times. 80 sts rem.

ROW 2 & ALL WS ROWS: Purl in shade A.

ROW 3: Using shade A [k2tog, k6] 10 times. 70 sts rem.

ROW 5: Using shade B, [k2tog, k5] 10 times. 60 sts rem.

ROW 7: Using shade B, [k2tog, k4] 10 times. 50 sts rem.

ROW 9: Using shade B, [k2tog, k3] 10 times. 40 sts rem.

ROW 11: Using shade B, [k2tog, k2] 10 times. 30 sts rem.

ROW 13: Using shade B, [k2tog] 15 times. 15 sts rem.

ROW 14: Using shade A, p2tog to last st, p1. 8 sts rem.

Break yarn and thread through rem sts, pull tight to draw together.

MAKING UP

✳ Block the Fair Isle part lightly. Sew the buttons in place as indicated on the chart. Sew up the side seam neatly and sew in any loose ends.

Beanie

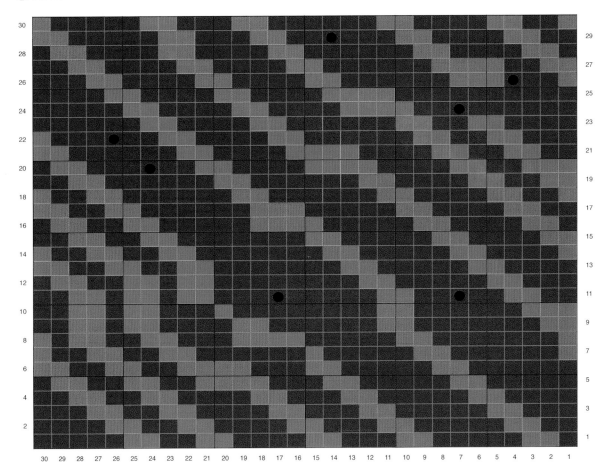

KEY

- ■ A
- ■ B
- ● BUTTON

MITTS

RIGHT HAND MITT

Using smaller needles and shade B, cast on 42 sts.

*Change to shade A.

ROW 1 [RS]: *K2, p2; rep from * to last 2 sts, k2.

ROW 2: *P2, k2; rep from * to last 2 sts, p2.

Rep the last 2 rows 6 more times, then work Row 1 once more.**

INC ROW [WS]: [P2, k2] 5 times, m1, *p2, k2; rep from * to last 2 sts, m1, p2. 44 sts.

Change to larger needles and beg with a RS row cont in St st, est chart as foll:

ROW 1: Beg at 1st st of Row 1, work the 23 sts from Mitts chart, using shade A, knit to end.

Work 3 more rows in St st changing colours as indicated.

THUMB GUSSET

ROW 5 [RS]: K23 sts from chart. Using shade A, m1, k2, m1, k19.

ROW 6 & EVERY WS ROW: Using A, purl to last 23 sts, p23 from chart.

ROW 7: K23 from chart. Using shade A, m1, k4, m1, k19. 48 sts.

ROW 9: K23 from chart. Using shade A, m1, k6, m1, k19. 50 sts.

ROW 11: K23 from chart. Using shade A, m1, k8, m1, k19. 52 sts

ROW 13: K23 from chart, m1, k10, m1, k19. 54 sts.

ROW 15: K23 from chart, m1, k12, m1, k19. 56 sts.

ROW 16 [WS]: P33, turn.

Mitts

KEY
- ■ A
- ■ B
- ● BUTTON

THUMB

NEXT ROW: Using A only, use the backwards loop method to cast on 2 sts, knit across 2 cast on sts and 14 sts for thumb, turn. 16 sts.

NEXT ROW: Use the backwards loop method to cast on 2 sts, purl across 2 cast on sts and 16 sts for thumb, turn. 18 sts.

Beg with a RS row, cont in St st on these 18 sts only for 4 rows.

Beg with row 1 of k2, p2 rib pattern work 3 rows even.

Using shade B, cast off loosely in rib.

Sew up thumb seam.

HAND

With WS facing, rejoin yarn to rem sts and purl to end as est.

ROW 17 (RS): Work as est to thumb, pick up and knit 4 sts across thumb cast on, work to end as est. 46 sts.

Cont working in patt as set until all 28 rows of chart are completed, ending with a WS row.

NEXT ROW (RS): Using shade A, *k2, p2; rep from * to last 2 sts, k2.

Work 2 more rows in k2, p2 rib as est.

Using shade B, cast off loosely in rib.

LEFT HAND MITT

Using smaller needles and shade B cast on 42 sts.

Work as for right hand mitt from * to **.

INC ROW: [P2, k2] 16 times, m1, *p2, k2 to last 2 sts, m1, p2. 44 sts.

Change to larger needles and beg with a RS row, cont in St st, est chart as foll:

ROW 1 (RS): K21, beg at 1st st of Row 1 of chart B k to end.

Work 3 more rows in St st, changing colours as indicated.

THUMB GUSSET

ROW 5 (RS): Using shade A, k19, m1, k2, m1, k23 from chart. 48 sts.

ROW 6 & EVERY WS ROW: P23 from chart, using shade A, purl to end.

ROW 7: Using shade A, k19, m1, k4, m1, k23 from chart. 48 sts.

ROW 9: Using shade A, k19, m1, k6, m1, k23 from chart. 50 sts.

ROW 11: Using shade A, k19, m1, k8, m1, k23 from chart. 52 sts.

ROW 13: Using shade A, k19, m1, k10, m1, k23 from chart. 54 sts.

ROW 15: Using shade A, k19, m1, k12, m1, k23 from chart. 56 sts.

ROW 16: P37, turn.

THUMB

Complete as for right-hand mitt to end.

MAKING UP

✳ Sew on the buttons positioning them as shown on the chart.

✳ Sew in loose ends and sew up side seams.

TIP: INSTEAD OF USING THE BUTTONS FOR EMBELLISHMENT SEW FRENCH KNOTS USING A BRIGHT YELLOW SHADE.

MEN'S RADIO MAST
Socks

Radio masts were designed to support aerials for broadcasting radio and TV. They are exceptionally tall and the elegant latticework structure has been reproduced as a graphic image in various formats over the years, appearing on many logos. This interpretation works as a one-colour design on a pair of socks knitted using the Fair Isle method. The socks are knitted on a set of five double-pointed needles, but a short circular needle can be used if preferred. For a hard-wearing pair of socks choose a specialized sock yarn that is machine washable and has a 20% nylon content.

MATERIALS

YARN: 4-ply.

Shown here: Mini Mochi Solid sock yarn (80% merino wool, 20% nylon; 178m (195yd)/50g): deep loden (A), 2 (2, 3) balls; natural ecru (B), 1 (1, 1) ball.

NEEDLES: 2.5mm: double-pointed needles (dpns).

Adjust needle size if needed to obtain tension.

HABERDASHERY: Stitch marker (m), stitch holder, tapestry needle.

TENSION: 32 sts and 48 rnds to 10cm (4") in St st.

SIZES: 21.5 (23.5, 25.5)cm (8½ (9¼, 10)") foot circumference.

SCORE: 60 POINTS

PATTERN *Note*

The round change is between needles 4 and 1. The last st on needle 4 is the centre back stitch, mark this with a stitch marker at all times if you prefer to work with circular needles.

RIGHT SOCK

Using shade A and one needle cast on 68 (76, 80) sts, divide sts evenly over 4 dpns, join to work in rnds being careful not to twist sts and cont in k2, p2 rib as foll:

RND 1: *K2, p2; rep from * to end.

Rep Rnd 1 for a total of 14 rnds.

NEXT RND: Sizes 21.5 (25.5) cm only: Inc Rnd – M1, knit to end. 69 (81) sts.

Size 23.5cm only: Dec Rnd – K2tog, knit to end. 75 sts rem.

All Sizes: Cont in St st for 4 more rnds. *

EST CHART: Using shade A, k1 (2, 3), work 31 sts from chart changing colours as indicated. Using shade A, k37 (42:47).

This sets the position of chart, cont until all 39 rows of chart have been worked.

** Work 11 rnds in St st.

HEEL FLAP

ROW 1 [RS]: K9 sts from ndl 1, turn.

ROW 2: P9 sts from ndl 1, p10 sts from ndl 4. 19 sts.

Cont on these 19 sts only, leaving rem 50 (56, 62) sts on a holder.

ROW 3: Sl 1 pwise wyb, knit to end.

ROW 4: Sl 1 pwise wyf, purl to end. Rep the last 2 rows 12 more times.

TURN HEEL

ROW 1 [RS]: K14, turn.

ROW 2: P9, turn.

ROW 3: K8, skp, k1, turn.

ROW 4: P9, p2tog, p1, turn.

ROW 5: K10, skp, k1, turn.

ROW 6: P11, p2tog, p1, turn.

ROW 7: K12, skp, turn.

ROW 8: P12, skp, turn. 13 sts.

Radio Mast Socks

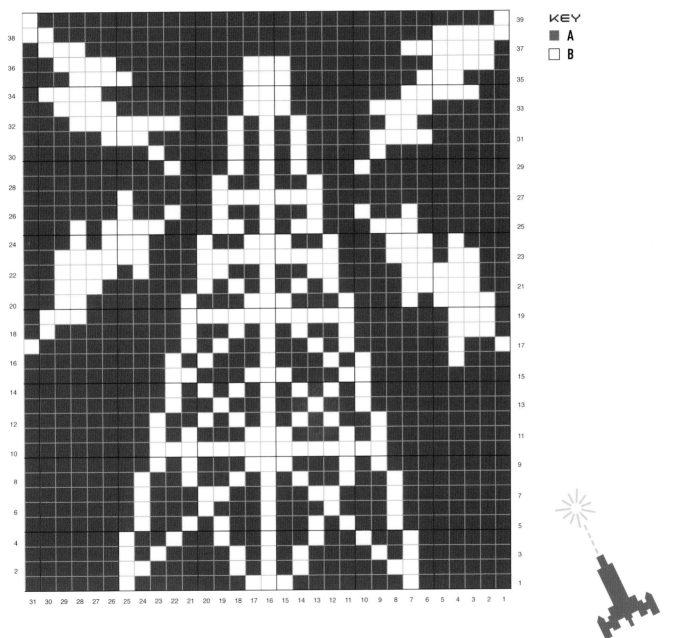

KEY
- ▦ A
- ☐ B

GUSSET

RND 1: K6, pm, k1 (this 1st is the centre back st).

Change to new needle (this will become needle 1).

K6, pick up and knit 15 sts down side of heel flap, return 50 (56, 62) held sts onto dpns, and k2 (3, 5) – 23 (24, 26) sts ndl 1.

Change to new needle k17 (19, 20) for instep. 17 (19, 20) sts ndl 2.

Change to new needle k17 (19, 20) for instep. 17 (19, 20) sts ndl 3.

Change to new needle, k2 (3, 5), pick up and knit 15 sts up side of heel flap, knit rem 7 sts (keeping marker in place). 24 (25, 27) sts ndl 4.

Cont working in rnds as foll:
RND 2: On ndl 1 – knit to last 3 sts, k2tog, k1; on ndls 2 and 3: knit; on ndl 4: k1, skp, knit to end. 2 sts dec'd.

NEXT RND: K to end.

Rep last 2 rnds 5 more times. 69 (75, 81) sts rem.

Cont working in rnds until foot measures 21.5 (22, 24)cm from heel.

Ensure that the stitches are split evenly over the four dpns 17 (18, 20) sts on ndl 1; 17 (19, 20) sts on ndls 2 and 3, and 18 (19, 21) sts on ndl 4 with the marked st at the end of ndl 4.

TOE SHAPING

RND 1: On ndls 1 and 3 – knit to last 3 sts, k2tog, k1; on ndls 2 and 4: k1, skp, knit to end. 4 sts dec'd.

RND 2: Knit.

Rep these 2 rnds 14 (15, 16) more times. 9 (11, 13) sts rem.

Break yarn, thread tail end onto a needle, pass through the 9 (11, 13) sts and draw tight. Fasten on the inside of the sock.

LEFT SOCK

Work same as for right sock to *.

EST CHART: K37 (42, 47), work 31 sts from chart changing colours as indicated, k1 (2, 3).

Cont as est until all 39 rows of chart have been worked.

Continue same as right sock from ** to end.

MAKING UP

✳ Sew in any loose ends, block and press lightly.

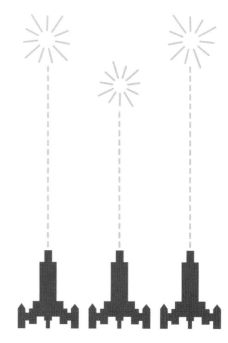

TIP: IF YOU WANT TO MAKE A LONGER PAIR OF SOCKS, ADD IN AS MANY EXTRA ROWS AS YOU LIKE BEFORE THE HEEL SHAPING.

CIRCUIT BOARD
Scarf

Knit the circuit board scarf to complete the hat and beanie set. This luxuriously soft scarf is designed to wear knotted around the neck. It is knitted using the Fair Isle method and the button embellishments are sewn on afterwards.

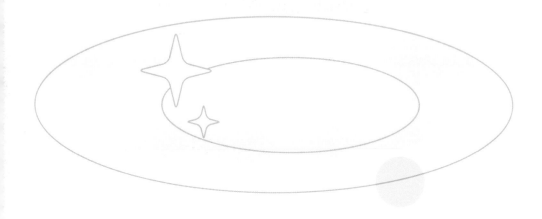

MATERIALS

YARN: Aran weight.

Shown here: Debbie Bliss Cashmerino Aran (55% merino wool, 33% microfibre, 12% cashmere; 90m (98yd)/50g): kahki (A), 3 balls; lime green (B), 1 ball.

NEEDLES: 5.5mm: straight.
HABERDASHERY: 99 small buttons, tapestry needle. Adjust needle size if necessary to obtain correct tension.

TENSION: 19 sts and 24 rows to 10cm (4") in pattern.

FINISHED MEASUREMENT: About 18cm (7") wide x 155cm (60") long.

SCORE: 55 POINTS

PATTERN *Note*

The length of the scarf can easily be increased, each pattern rep of 40 rows measures 17cm (6¾"). Alternatively make tassels using shade B and attach them to each end of the scarf.

SCARF

Using shade A, cast on 34 sts.

Knit 2 rows.

Working in St st throughout cont as foll:

ROW 1 (RS): With shade A, k2, knit the 30 sts from chart, reading chart from right to left on RS rows and from left to right on WS rows. With shade A, k2.

ROW 2 (WS): With shade A, k2, purl the 30 sts from chart, k2.

These 2 rows est the pattern. Cont changing colours as indicated and working the first and last 2 sts of every row in garter st until 9 pattern reps have been worked (360 rows from garter st edge).

Knit 2 rows.

Cast off.

MAKING UP

✻ Sew in any loose ends, block to measurements.

✻ Sew on the buttons in the positions indicated on the chart.

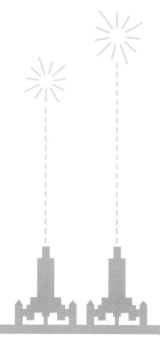

TIP: FOR A TEXTURED EFFECT, KNIT THE SCARF IN JUST ONE SHADE, WORKING THE SYMBOLS ON THE CHART IN REVERSE ST ST.

Circuit Board Scarf

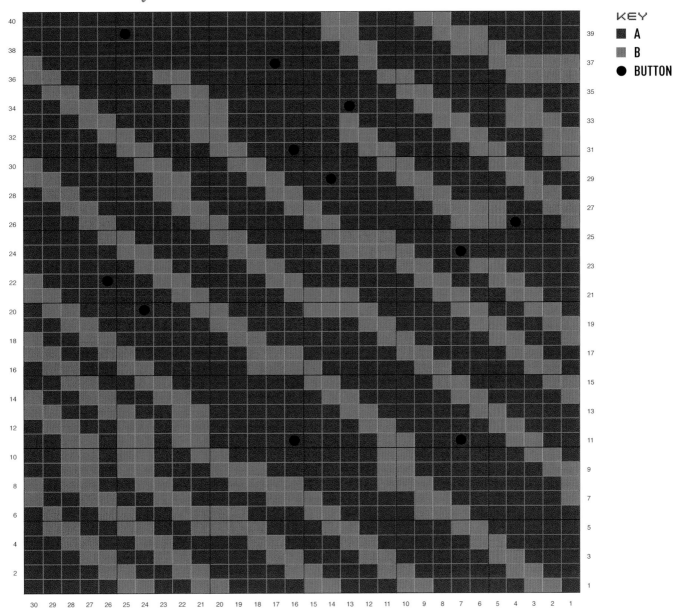

KEY

■ A
■ B
● BUTTON

ROBOT CUSHION
Cover

Combining space-age with modern living, these colourful robots will appeal to all ages. Use the design in a child's bedroom or decorate a sofa with four or five cushions in contrasting colours. The colourful robots stand out on the dark background, but try changing the colours to suit your own décor. The cushion cover is knitted using the Fair Isle method and is fastened at the back with a row of buttons so that it can be removed for washing.

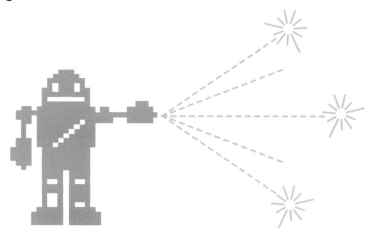

MATERIALS

YARN: DK weight (#3 Light).

Shown here: Debbie Bliss Railto (100% extra fine merino wool; 105m (115yd)/50g): black (A), 3 balls; blue (B), pink (C) and green (D), 1 ball each.

NEEDLES: 3.75 and 4mm: straight.

Adjust needle sizes if necessary to obtain correct tension.

HABERDASHERY: 5 buttons, 40.5cm (16") square pillow form, tapestry needle.

TENSION: 22 sts and 26.5 rows to 10cm (4") in Fair Isle pattern using larger needles.

FINISHED MEASUREMENT: About 40.5cm (16") square.

SCORE: 70 POINTS

PATTERN *Note*

Read the charts from right to left on the RS rows and from left to right on the WS rows weaving the colours at the back over 3 sts.

BOTTOM BACK

Using shade A and smaller needles cast on 86 sts.

Beg and end with a RS row work 9 rows in St st.

NEXT ROW (WS): P1, m1p, purl to last st, m1p, p1. 88 sts.

Change to larger needles and cont in St st throughout.

Est Robot Chart A as foll:

ROW 1 (RS): With shade A, k, *work 19 sts from chart A. With shade A, k2; rep from * to last st. With shade A, k1.

ROW 2 (WS): With shade A, p2, *work 19 sts from Robot chart A, with shade A, p2; rep from * to last st. With shade A, p1.

Cont changing colours as indicated until all 30 rows of the chart have been worked.

Change to smaller needles and shade A only.

DEC ROW (RS): K1, k2tog, knit to last 3 sts, skp, k1. 86 sts.

Beg and end with a WS row, work 3 rows in St st.

BUTTONHOLE BORDER
ROW 1 (RS): *K2, p2; rep from * to last 2 sts, k2.

ROW 2: *P2, k2; rep from * to last 2 sts, p2.

Rep the last 2 rows 3 more times.

ROW 9 (BUTTONHOLE ROW): K2, p2, k2, [cast off 2, work 16 sts as est] 4 times, cast off 2, k2, p2, k2.

ROW 10: P2, k2, p2 [use the backwards loop method to cast on 2, work 16 sts as est] 4 times, cast on 2, p2, k2, p2.

Work 6 more rows in k2, p2 rib patt as est.

Cast off in rib.

TOP BACK

Using shade A and smaller needles, cast on 86 sts.

ROW 1 (RS): *K2, p2; rep from * to last 2 sts, k2.

Robot A

Robot B

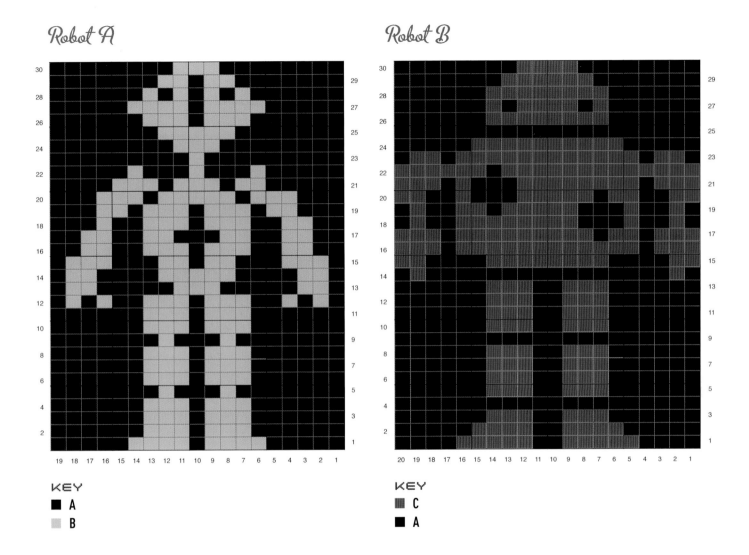

KEY
- ■ A
- ■ B

KEY
- ▨ C
- ■ A

TIP: CHANGE THE COLOUR SCHEME TO MATCH YOUR DÉCOR, OR, IF YOU WANT TO INCREASE THE SIZE OF THE COVER, CAST ON AN EXTRA 14 STS FOR EVERY 5CM (2") INCREMENT, PLUS 2 EXTRA STS TO KEEP THE 2X2 RIB PATTERN CORRECT.

Robot C

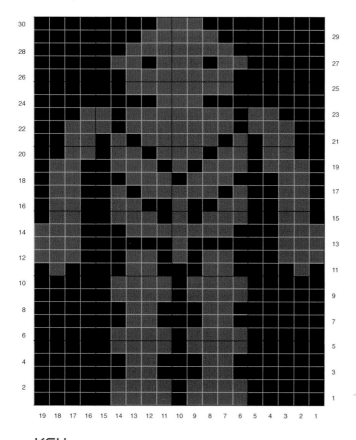

KEY
- ■ C
- ■ A

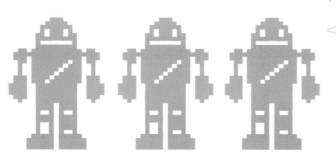

ROW 2: *P2, k2; rep from * to last 2 sts, p2.

Rep the last 2 rows 7 more times.

Beg and end with a RS row work 3 rows in St st.

INC ROW [WS]: P1, m1p, purl to last st, m1p, p1. 88 sts.

Change to 4mm needles and cont in St st throughout.

Est Robot Chart C as foll:

ROW 1 [RS]: With shade A, k3, *work 19 sts from Robot chart C. With shade B, k2; rep from * to last st, with shade B, k1.

ROW 2 [WS]: With shade A, p3 *work 19 sts from Robot chart C. With shade A, p2; rep from * to last st, with shade A, p1.

Cont changing colours as indicated until all 30 rows of the chart have been worked.

Change to smaller needles and A only.

DEC ROW [RS]: K1, k2tog, knit to last 3 sts, skp, k1. 86 sts.

Beg and end with a WS row, work 9 rows in St st.

Cast off.

FRONT

Using shade A and smaller needles, cast on 86 sts.

Beg and end with a RS row work 9 rows in St st.

NEXT ROW (WS): P1, m1p, purl to last st, m1p, p1. 88 sts.

Change to larger needles and cont in St st throughout.

Est Robot Chart A as foll:

ROW 1 (RS): With shade A, k3, *work 19 sts from Robot chart A. With shade B k2; rep from * to last st, with shade A, k1.

ROW 2 (WS): With shade A, p3 *work 19 sts from chart A. With shade A, p2; rep from * to last st, with shade A, p1.

Cont changing colours as indicated until 28 rows of chart have been worked.

Place row 1 of Robot chart B as foll:

NEXT ROW: K10A, 2B, 1A, 2B, *2A, 5C, 2A, 5B, 2A, 2B, 1A, 2B; rep from * to last 10 sts, k10A.

Work the final row of Robot chart A and second row of Robot chart B. Cont until 28 rows of Robot chart C have been worked.

Place row 1 of Robot chart C as foll:

NEXT ROW: K8A, 4D, 1A, 4D, *3A, 6C, 3A, 4D, 1A, 4D; rep from * to last 8 sts, k8A.

Work the final row of Robot chart B and second row of Robot chart C.

Cont until all 30 rows of chart C have been worked.

Change to smaller needles and shade A only.

DEC ROW (RS): K1, k2tog, knit to last 3 sts, skp, k1. 86 sts.

Beg and end with a WS row, work 9 rows in St st.

Cast off.

MAKING UP

※ Sew in any loose ends, block and press the three pieces.

※ Lay down the front with RS facing up; place the bottom back RS together with front lining up cast on edges. Place the top back RS together with front lining up cast off edges and overlapping the ribs. Pin together and stitch all the seams.

※ Turn RS outward and sew on the buttons to correspond with the buttonholes.

SPUTNIK LAPTOP
Cover

Sputnik 1 is the classic symbol of the Space Age and the wonderful graphic image makes a perfect laptop cover. It was the first artificial satellite to be put into Earth's orbit, heralding the start of the space race and, although it was only in space for a few months, it presents an image that is instantly recognizable. The design is knitted in cotton using the intarsia method and worked in stocking stitch and garter stitch. The felt fabric lining helps to give extra protection and the cover is fastened at the front with a row of buttons.

MATERIALS

YARN: DK weight.

Shown here: Rowan Cotton Glacé (100% cotton; 126m (115yd)/50g): poppy (red) (A) 3 balls; ecru (B), 1 ball.

NEEDLES: 2.75 and 3.25mm: straight.

Adjust needle sizes if necessary to obtain correct tension.

HABERDASHERY: 2.75mm crochet hook, 6 buttons, 26.5cm (10½") x 75cm (29½") piece of felt fabric for lining, sewing needle and thread, tapestry needle.

TENSION: 23 sts and 32 rows to 10cm (4") in St st using larger needles.

– – – – – – – – – – – – – – – – –

FINISHED MEASUREMENT: About 28cm (11") wide x 33cm (13") tall.

SCORE: 40 POINTS

PATTERN *Note*

The cover is made in one piece starting at the base of the front flap and the chart is worked from right to left on RS rows and from left to right on WS rows.

COVER

FRONT FLAP

Using smaller needles and shade A cast on 66 sts.

ROW 1 (RS): K6, p2, *k2, p2; rep from * to last 6 sts, k6.

ROW 2: K4, *p2, k2; rep from * to last 6 sts, p2, k4.

Rep rows the last 2 rows 3 more times, then row 1 once more.

NEXT ROW (WS): Knit.

Using larger needles and beg with a RS row, cont to work in St st, keeping the garter st edging est as foll:

ROW 1 (RS): With shade A, k7. Work the 51 sts of chart, k8.

ROW 2: K4, p4, work next row of chart, p3, k4.

Cont as above working the 4 edge sts in garter st and keeping the chart placement as est until all 79 rows of the chart have been worked.

ROW 80: K4, purl to last 4 sts, k4.

ROW 81: Knit.

ROW 82: Rep row 80.

BACK AND FLAP

NEXT ROW: Cont in shade A, work in garter st until work measures 76cm (30") from cast on edge.

Cast off.

Sputnik Laptop Cover

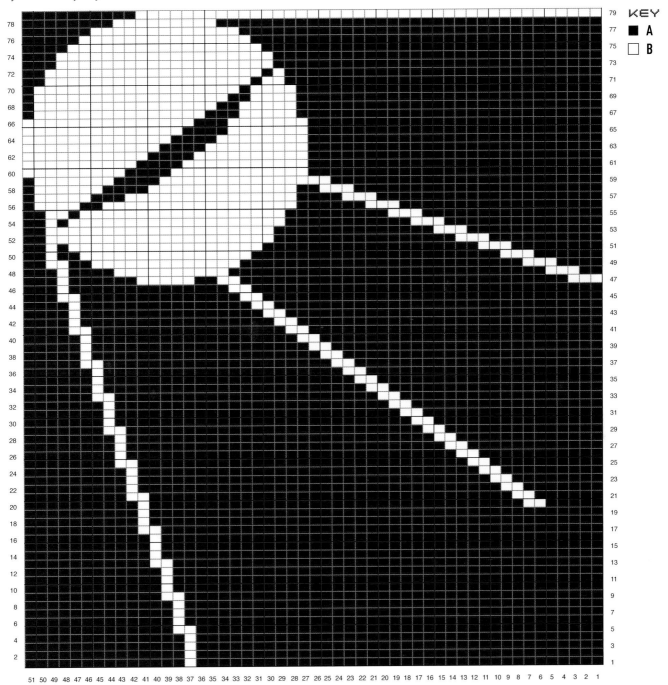

KEY

■ A

□ B

MAKING UP

❋ Block and press the knitted piece.

❋ If necessary cut the lining fabric to make it 1.3cm (½") smaller than the knitted piece all round.

❋ Place the lining fabric and knitted piece WS together and neatly slip stitch all the way around the edge.

BUTTONHOLES

With RS of front flap facing, using yarn A and crochet hook work along cast on edge as foll:

ROW 1 [RS]: Ch 1, sc into next and every foll st to end of row, turn. 66 sts.

ROW 2: Ch 1, sc into 1st st, [ch 3, sk 3 sts, sc 9] 5 times, ch 3, sk 3 sts, sc 2. Fasten off.

Lay the cover flat with the fabric side facing up and front flap at the top. Fold up 10cm (4") of the bottom flap and sew the two short side seams to the back, fold the front cover down so that the ribbed edging overlaps the bottom flap by 7.5cm (3"), stitch the two long side seams to the back.

Fasten the buttons on the bottom flap to correspond with the buttonholes.

TIP: TO MAKE THE COVER LARGER, INCREASE THE NUMBER OF STITCHES CAST ON, WORKING EQUAL NUMBERS EACH SIDE OF THE CHART. INCREASE THE LENGTH BY WORKING EXTRA ROWS BEFORE AND AFTER THE CHART AND ON THE BACK.

ROBOT
Doorstop

Robots are famous for being handy around the house so what better way to stop your door from slamming than wedging it open with a chunky robot. This 3D robot is knitted in hard-wearing denim yarn and then stuffed with a combination of dried beans and toy stuffing. The denim yarn is perfect for the job, but if brighter colours are wanted swap this for a double knit cotton and make it to the measurements given after washing. The design can be knitted using the Fair Isle method or by Swiss darning it after knitting.

MATERIALS

YARN: Aran weight.

Shown here: Rowan Denim (100% cotton; 109m (100yd)/50g): ecru (A), 2 balls; Memphis (B), 1 ball.

NEEDLES: Size U.S. 6 (4mm): straight.

Adjust needle size if necessary to obtain correct tension.

HABERDASHERY: Small piece of blue felt, 2 small blue buttons, toy stuffing, dry rice or beans, scissors, tapestry needle.

TENSION: Before washing 20 sts and 28 rows to 10cm (4") in St st.

After washing 20 sts and 32 rows to 10cm (4") in St st.

MEASUREMENT: 28cm (11") tall from base to top of head x 12.5cm (5") wide x 5cm (2") deep (after washing).

SCORE: 35 POINTS

PATTERN Note

The robot is knitted in six pieces; these are machine washed before sewing up and will shrink in length (see ball band of yarn for further details).

BACK

Using shade A, cast on 25 sts.

Beg with a RS row, work in St st for 70 rows.

Cast off 5 sts at the beg of next 2 rows. 15 sts rem.

Cont in St st for a further 18 rows.

Cast off rem sts.

FRONT

Work same as back, working in St st throughout, at the same time placing the chart designs as foll:

ROWS 1–4: Work chart A.

ROWS 5–34: Work 12A, 1B, 12A.

ROW 35: Knit using shade B.

ROW 36: Purl using shade A.

ROWS 37–66: Work chart B.

ROWS 67–70: Work in St st using shade A.

ROW 71: Using shade A, cast off 5 sts, knit to end. 20 sts.

ROW 72: Using shade A, cast off 5 sts, p to end. 15 sts.

ROWS 73–89: Work from chart C.

Cast off rem sts.

SIDE PANEL

Using shade A cast on 12 sts.

Beg with a k row, work in St st for 180 rows (this should reach all the way around the edge of the robot front when stretched slightly).

Cast off.

BASE

Using shade A cast on 25 sts.

Beg with a RS row, work 20 rows in St st.

Cast off.

ARMS

(Make 2)

Using shade A cast on 14 sts.

Beg with a RS row, work 26 rows in St st.

NEXT ROW: Use the backwards loop method to cast on 4 sts, work to the end of the row cast on 4 sts. 22 sts.

Work 9 rows in St st ending with a WS row.

NEXT ROW (RS): K11, fold work in half so that both needle tips are pointing in same direction. Cast off 11 sts using the 3-needle cast-off method.

TIP: FOR A MORE ANGULAR FINISH, STUFF THE HEAD AND ARMS WITH TOY STUFFING BUT USE A BRICK OR BLOCK OF WOOD FOR THE MAIN BODY.

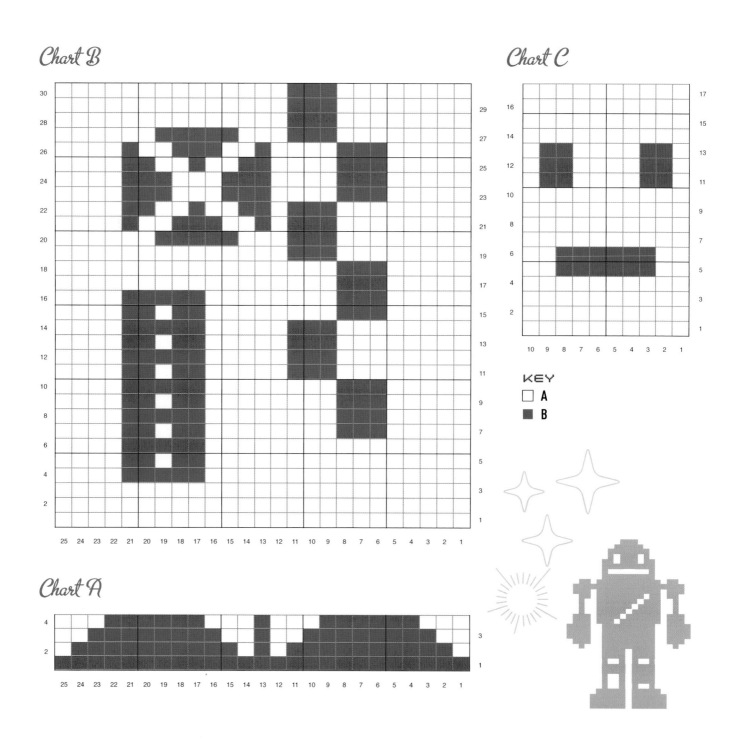

Chart B

Chart C

KEY

- ☐ A
- ■ B

Chart A

MAKING UP

❋ Sew in any loose ends. Work any Swiss darning before washing. Machine wash all the pieces before sewing up (see ball band for instructions).

❋ Placing RS together pin the side panel all round the edge of front of robot easing it in place, stitch using back stitch. Attach the back of the robot to the side panel in the same way.

❋ Stuff the head firmly with toy stuffing.

❋ Sew the base on to the bottom of the robot leaving one side edge open. Stuff the body with a mix of toy stuffing and rice, sew up the remaining seam on the base.

❋ Sew the side seams of the arms, leaving an opening. Stuff with toy stuffing and attach to the body.

❋ Cut out two large discs and two small discs from the felt, attach one large disc, one small one and a button to each side of the head.

❋ To make the robot 'claw', cut out 4 equal crescent shapes from the felt. Sew two pieces together for each claw and attach to the bottom of the arms.

RAY GUN
Place Mat & Coaster

Ray guns, although completely fictional, conjure up fond memories of old comic strips and sci-fi films when every baddie carried one. Relive this experience at the dining room table with a trip down memory lane for the adults and a bit of fun for the kids. A matching set of place mats and coasters will make meal times enjoyable. These durable mats are knitted in a cotton denim yarn that can be washed regularly.

MATERIALS

YARN: Aran weight

Shown here: Rowan Denim (100% cotton; 109m (100yd)/50g): Nashville (A), 2 balls; Tennessee (B) and ecru (C), 1 ball each.

NEEDLES: 4mm: straight.

Adjust needle size if necessary to obtain correct tension.

HABERDASHERY:

Tapestry needle.

- -

TENSION: Before washing 20 sts and 28 rows using 10cm (4") in pattern. After washing 20 sts and 32 rows =10cm (4") in pattern.

- -

FINISHED MEASUREMENTS:
(after washing)

PLACE MAT About 33cm (13") wide x 24cm (9½") tall.

COASTER About 12.5cm (5") wide x 12cm (4¾") tall.

SCORE: 65 POINTS

PATTERN Note

The designs are worked using the intarsia method; wind off small balls of yarn to use for each section of colour.

PLACE MAT

Using shade A, cast on 65 sts.

ROW 1: *K1, p1; rep from * to last st, k1.

Rep last row 3 more times.

ROW 5 (RS): K1, p1, knit to last 2 sts, p1, k1.

ROW 6: K1, p1, k1, purl to last 3 sts, k1, p1, k1.

Rep last 2 rows 8 more times.

NEXT ROW: Using shade A, k1, p1, k13, work 35 sts of Place Mat chart, changing colours as indicated. Using shade A, k13, p1, k1.

NEXT ROW: Using shade A, k1, p1, k1, p12, work the 35 sts of Place Mat chart, changing colours as indicated. Using shade A, p12, k1, p1, k1.

Cont to work the Place Mat chart from right to left on the RS and from left to right on the WS of work. AT THE SAME TIME cont to work the moss st edging at each end of the row as est.

When the 36 rows of the Place Mat chart have been completed, cont in St st working the moss st edging at each end of every row for 18 rows.

NEXT ROW: *K1, p1, rep from * to last st, k1.

Rep last row 3 more times.

Cast off in moss st.

COASTER

Using shade A, cast on 25 sts.

ROW 1: *K1, p1, rep from * to last st, k1.

Rep last row 2 more times.

NEXT ROW (WS): K1, purl to last st, k1.

NEXT ROW (RS): K1, p1, work the 21 sts of the Coaster chart, changing colours as indicated, p1, k1.

Place Mat

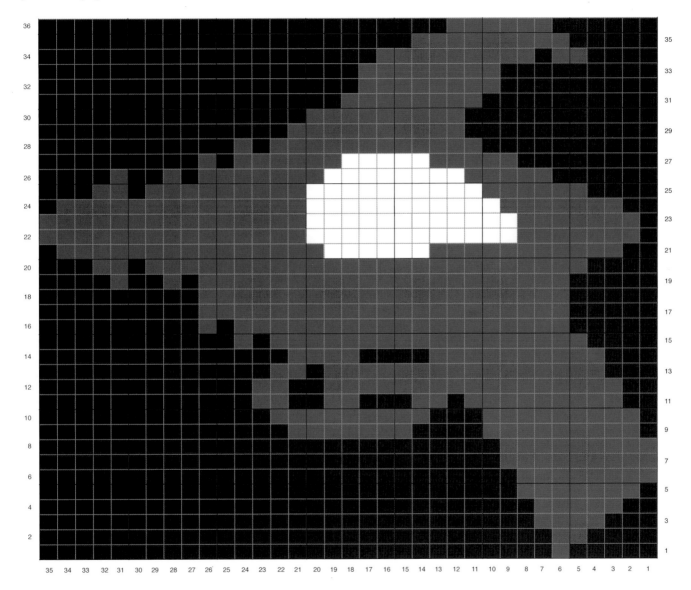

KEY
■ A ■ B □ C

Coaster

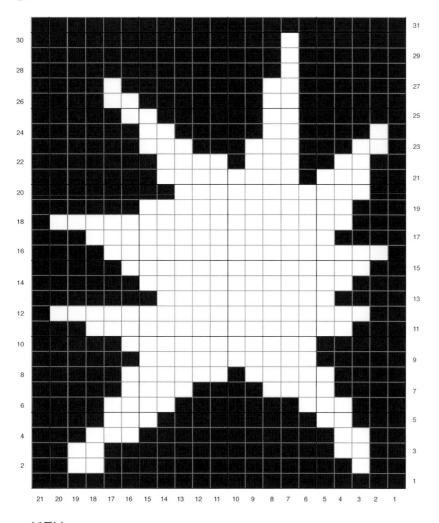

KEY

■ A ☐ C

NEXT ROW: K1, p1, work the 21 sts of the Coaster chart pattern changing colours as indicated, p1, k1.

Cont to work the Coaster chart from right to left on the RS and from left to right on the WS of work. AT THE SAME TIME cont to work the moss st edging at each end of the row as set.

When the 31 rows of the Coaster chart have been worked cont as foll:

NEXT ROW: *K1, p1, rep from * to last st, k1.

Rep last row 2 more times.

Cast off in moss st.

MAKING UP

✳ Sew in any loose ends. Wash both pieces in the washing machine as instructed, while still damp pin out to shape ensuring the edges are straight and leave to dry.

TIP: THE MATS CAN BE KNITTED IN ORDINARY DK-WEIGHT COTTON, BUT REMEMBER THE FINISHED MEASUREMENT WILL BE LARGER.

HEADPHONES
Hat

Pop on the cans and pump up the volume. A classic set of headphones are the perfect shape to be transformed into a hat – the cans fit over the earflaps giving a cosy finish. It is knitted in soft pure wool in cool neutral shades that will go with anything. The pattern is stocking stitch all the way, using the intarsia method for the design and a simple crochet edging.

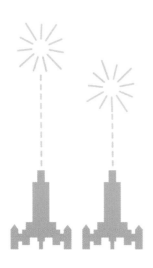

MATERIALS

YARN: Aran weight.

Shown here: Debbie Bliss Rialto Aran (100 % extrafine merino wool 80m (88yd)/ 50g): light grey (A), charcoal grey (B) and black (C), 1 ball each.

NEEDLES: 5mm: straight and two double-pointed.

Adjust needle size if necessary to obtain the correct tension.

HABERDASHERY:

4.5mm crochet hook, tapestry needle.

- - - - - - - - - - - - - - - - - -

TENSION: 18 sts and 28 rows to 10cm (4") in St st.

- - - - - - - - - - - - - - - - - -

FINISHED MEASUREMENTS:
16.5cm (6½") from front edge to crown x 51cm (20") in circumference (will stretch to fit a head measuring about 58.5cm (23") circumference).

SCORE: 50 POINTS

PATTERN *Note*

Rows 1–10 of the chart are worked only in the contrast shades; the charted design shows the shaping for the earflaps to row 10, from row 11 onwards there is no further shaping. For colour changes use the intarsia method throughout.

EAR FLAPS

(Make two)

Using shade C, cast on 7 sts.

Beg at Row 1 and st 6 of chart and changing colours as indicated cont as folls:

ROW 1 (RS): Using shade C only, k7.

ROW 2 & EVERY WS ROW: Purl.

ROW 3: K1, m1, k5, m1, k1. 9 sts.

ROW 5: K1, m1, k7, m1, k1. 11 sts.

ROW 7: K1, m1, k9, m1, k1. 13 sts.

ROW 9: K1, m1, k11, m1, k1. 15 sts.

ROW 11: K1, m1, k13, m1, k1. 17 sts.

Cont on these 17 sts working

pattern as set from chart and changing colours as indicated until row 26 of chart has been worked.

Cut yarn, leave sts on a dpn and make second ear flap in the same way.

MAIN PART

With RS of ear flaps facing cont as folls:

ROW 27 (RS): Using shade A cast on 12 sts, work row 27 of chart across the 17 sts of first ear flap changing colours as indicated, using shade A and the backwards loop method to cast on 32 sts, work row 27 of chart across 17 sts of second ear flap, use A and the backwards loop method to cast on 12 sts. 90 sts.

ROW 28: Purl across all sts keeping in pattern on the 17 sts above ear flap and working rem sts in shade A.

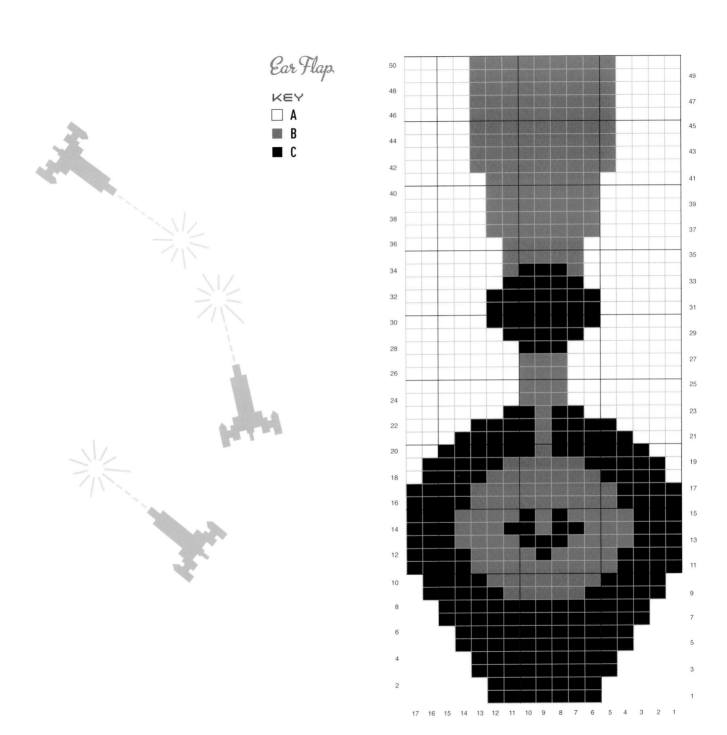

Ear Flap

KEY

□ A

▨ B

■ C

Cont on these 90 sts working the pattern panel as shown on the chart in shade B and the rem sts in shade A until all 50 rows of the chart have been completed.

SHAPING FOR CROWN

Keeping the colour change as est on the chart (the band will get narrower as you work the decreases) cont as folls:

ROW 51 (DEC): K14, k2tog, k9, k2tog, k36, k2tog, k9, k2tog, k14.

ROW 52 & EVERY WS ROW: Purl.

ROW 53: K13, k2tog, k9, k2tog, k34, k2tog, k9, k2tog, k13. 82 sts rem.

ROW 55: K12, k2tog, k9, k2tog, k32, k2tog, k9, k2tog, k12. 78 sts rem.

ROW 57: K11, k2tog, k9, k2tog, k30, k2tog, k9, k2tog, k11. 74 sts rem.

ROW 59: K10, k2tog, k9, k2tog, k28, k2tog, k9, k2tog, k10. 70 sts rem.

ROW 61: K9, k2tog, k9, k2tog, k26, k2tog, k9, k2tog, k9. 66 sts rem.

ROW 63: K8, k2tog, k9, k2tog; k24, k2tog, k9, k2tog, k8. 62 sts rem.

ROW 65: K2tog, *k3, k2tog; rep from * to end. 49 sts rem.

ROW 67: *K2, k2tog; rep from * to last st, k1. 37 sts rem.

ROW 69: K1, *k2tog, k1; rep from * to end. 25 sts rem.

ROW 71: K2tog to last st, k1. 13 sts.

Break yarn and thread through rem 13 sts, pull tight to draw together.

MAKING UP

❋ Block and press lightly.

❋ Sew up back seam neatly and sew in any loose ends.

❋ Using the crochet hook and shade B, beg at the back seam, work 2 rnds of sc around the base of the hat and each earflap.

❋ Fasten off and block again if necessary.

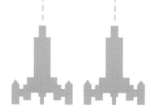

TIP: LIVEN IT UP BY ADDING A POMPOM TO THE TOP OF THE HAT AND TASSELS TO THE BOTTOM OF THE EARFLAPS.

CALCULATOR
Tablet Cover

A retro calculator makes the ideal cover for a tablet or netbook. This classic style is knitted using the Fair Isle and intarsia techniques in a soft cotton. The grid design is easy to knit and the numbers can be worked using the Fair Isle technique or by Swiss darning. It is fastened securely with press studs and can be lined with fabric for extra padding.

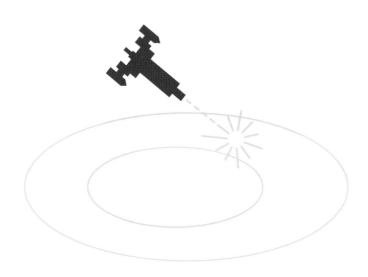

MATERIALS

YARN: Aran weight.

Shown here: Rowan Handknit Cotton (100% cotton; 93m (85yd)/50g): black (A), 2 balls; linen (B), bleached (C), rosso (red) (D) and Florence (orange) (E), 1 ball each.

NEEDLES: 3.75 and 4mm: straight.

Adjust needle sizes if necessary to obtain the correct tension.

HABERDASHERY: 3 press studs, tapestry needle.

TENSION: 20 sts and 26 rows to 10cm (4") in St st using larger needles.

FINISHED MEASUREMENT: About 30cm (12") long x 23.5cm (9") wide.

SCORE: 75 POINTS

PATTERN Note

The cover is worked in one piece starting at the base of the flap. It is knitted in St st using the Fair Isle method for the pattern stitches.

COVER

FRONT FLAP

Using smaller needles and shade A, cast on 44 sts.

Knit 4 rows.

Change to larger needles and cont as folls:

NEXT ROW [RS]: Knit.

NEXT ROW: K2, purl to last 2 sts, k2.

Cont to work in St st with 2 knit sts at each end of every WS row, and est chart as foll:

NEXT ROW [RS]: K2, changing colours as indicated and working Front Flap chart from right to left on RS rows and from left to right on WS rows, work the 40 st pattern, k2.

Cont as est until row 17 of the Front Flap chart has been worked.

TOP TURNING ROW

[WS]: Using shade A, knit to end.

BACK

NEXT ROW [RS]: Using shade A, knit to end.

NEXT ROW: Purl.

Beg and end with a RS row, cont in St st throughout, using shade A for 73 rows.

BASE TURNING ROW

[WS]: Using shade A, knit to end of row.

FRONT

NEXT ROW [RS]: K10, [m1, k8] 3 times, m1, k10. 48 sts.

NEXT ROW: Purl.

NEXT ROW: Using shade B, work the 53 rows of Calculator Tablet Cover chart, changing shades as indicated.

Beg with a WS row, cont in St st using shade B for 14 rows, ending with a RS row.

Knit 4 rows.

Cast off.

Front Flap

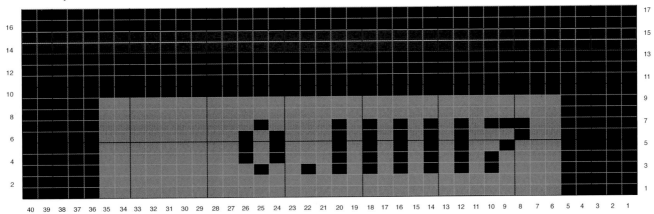

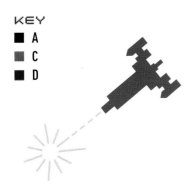

MAKING UP

✳ Fold the cover in half at the base turning row. Sew up the two side seams.

✳ Sew the press studs onto the inside of the flap spaced evenly along the garter st edging. Sew the other half of the press studs to the corresponding position on the front of the cover.

TIP: FOR EXTRA PROTECTION, MAKE A LINING FOR THE COVER. TAKE A PIECE OF FELT MEASURING TWICE THE LENGTH AND WIDTH OF THE KNITTED COVER, FOLD IN HALF SO THAT IT MEASURES THE SAME SIZE AS THE COVER. STITCH EACH SIDE SEAM AND PLACE THE LINING INSIDE THE COVER. STITCH THE TOP EDGE OF THE LINING TO THE INSIDE OF THE COVER.

Calculator Tablet Cover

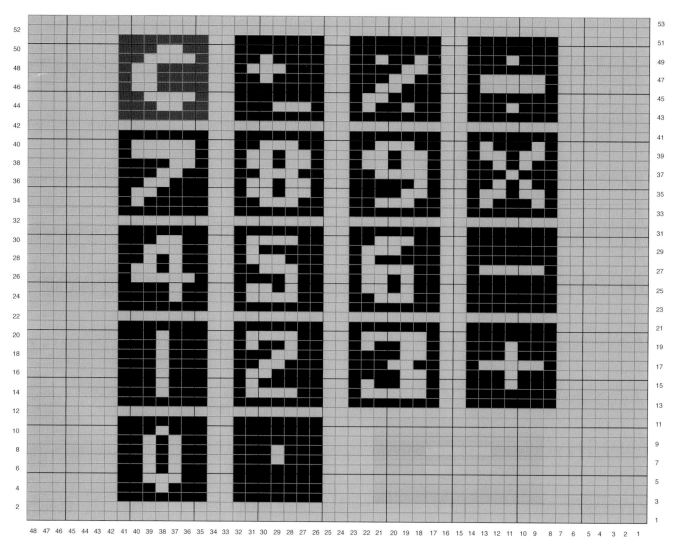

KEY
- ■ A
- ■ B
- ■ C
- ■ E

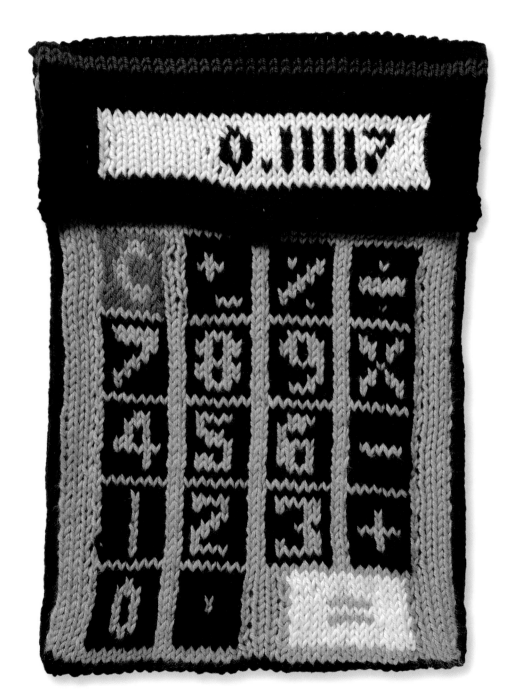

REEL-TO-REEL
Tote Bag

The reel-to-reel tape recorder was the predecessor to the cassette tape and, although a little bulky, produced high-quality recordings. There is something very satisfying about the image which conjures up nostalgic memories and makes a wonderful silhouette. The striking design for this tote bag is knitted using the intarsia method for the main body, the reels are knitted separately and worked in short row shaping, then attached to the bag with a button.

MATERIALS

YARN: Aran weight.

Shown here: Rowan Handknit Cotton (100% cotton; 93m (85yd)/50g): black (A), 5 balls; Florence (orange) (B), 2 balls; rosso (red) (C), 1 ball.

NEEDLES: 3.75 and 4mm: straight; 4mm: circular (cir).

Short 4mm circular needle.

Adjust needle sizes if necessary to obtain the correct tension.

HABERDASHERY: 2 large buttons, tapestry needle.

EXTRAS: 2 x large buttons.

- - - - - - - - - - - - - - - - - -

TENSION: 20 sts and 26 rows to 10cm (4") in St st using larger needles.

- - - - - - - - - - - - - - - - - -

FINISHED MEASUREMENTS:
About 35.5cm (14") wide x 35.5cm (14") high x 5cm (2") deep.

SCORE: 55 POINTS

PATTERN Note

The front and back of the bag are knitted in one, starting at the top edge of the back. Read the chart from right to left on the RS rows and from left to right on the WS rows.

BAG

BACK AND FRONT

Using shade A, and smaller needles, cast on 73 sts.

ROW 1: *K1, p1; rep from * to last st, k1.

This forms moss st. Rep the last row 5 more times.

Change to larger needles.

Beg and end with a RS row, cont in St st until work measures 35.5cm (14") from cast on.

TURNING ROW (WS): Knit.

Beg and end with a RS row work 11 rows in St st.

TURNING ROW (WS): Knit.

Beg with a RS row, work 4 rows in St st.

Est Chart as foll:

ROW 1: With shade A, k8, work 57 sts from chart changing colours as indicated. With shade A, k8.

ROW 2: With shade A, p8, work 57 sts from chart changing colours as indicated. With shade A, p8.

Cont as est until all 62 rows of chart have been worked.

Cont in St st using shade A only until front measures the same as back to beg of moss st band.

Change to smaller needles and work 6 rows in moss st.

Cast off.

SIDE PANELS

With RS of bag facing, pick up and knit 9 sts along along one side of the bag, between the two turning rows. Beg with a WS row, work in St st until side panel is the same length as front and back side edges to start of moss st band.

Work 6 rows in moss st, cast off.

Repeat on the other side of bag.

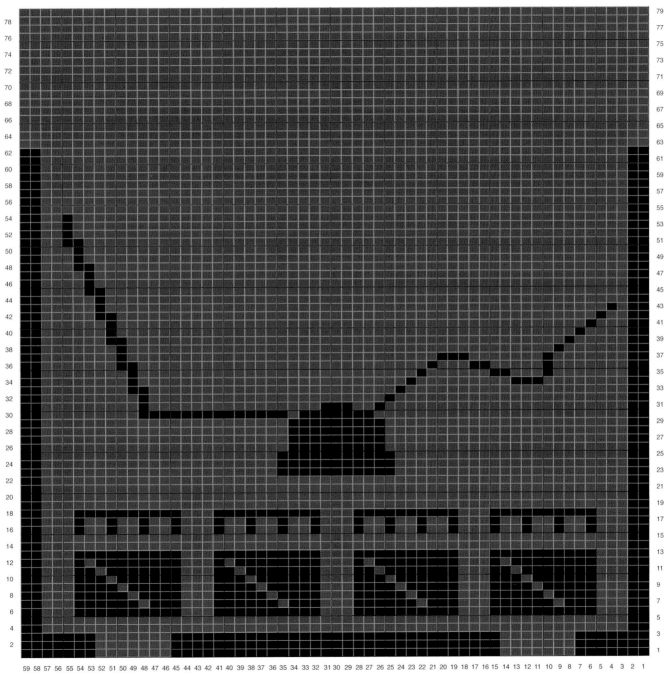

REELS

(Make 2)

Using shade A, cast on 18 sts.

ROW 1 (RS): Knit.

ROW 2: Purl.

ROWS 3 & 4: K15, turn, sl1 pwise wyf, purl to end.

ROWS 5 & 6: K13, turn, sl1 pwise wyf, purl to end.

ROWS 7 & 8: K11, turn, sl1 pwise wyf, purl to end.

ROWS 9 & 10: K9, turn sl1 pwise wyf, purl to end

ROWS 11 & 12: k7, turn, sl1 pwise wyf, purl to end.

ROWS 13 & 14: K5, turn, sl1 pwise wyf, purl to end.

ROWS 15 & 16: K3, turn, sl1 pwise wyf, purl to end.

ROW 17: K18.

ROW 18: Purl to end.

ROWS 19 & 20: K2A, k13C, turn, sl1 pwise wyf, p12C, p2A.

ROWS 21 & 22: K2A, k11C, turn, sl1 pwise wyf, p10C, p2A.

ROWS 23 & 24: K2A, k9C, turn, sl1 pwise wyf, p8C, p2A.

ROWS 25 & 26: K2A, k7C, turn, sl1 pwise wyf, p6C, p2A.

ROWS 27 & 28: K2A, k5C, turn, sl1 pwise wyf, p4C, p2A.

ROWS 29 & 30: K2A, k3C, turn, sl1, p2C, p2A.

ROWS 31 & 32: K2A, k1C, turn, sl1 pwise wyf, p2A.

Rep the last 32 rows 3 more times.

Cast off.

Sew the seam between the cast on and cast off edges.

Using larger circular needles and yarn B pick up and knit 120 sts around the outside edge of each reel.

Cast off.

HANDLES

(Make 2)

Using smaller needles and shade A, cast on 9 sts.

ROW 1: *K1, p1, rep from * to last st, k1.

Repeat this row until handle is 35.5cm (14") from cast on.

Cast off.

MAKING UP

❊ Sew the side panels onto the front and back of bag.

❊ Sew one handle on the front of bag 5cm (2") in from each side seam and the second handle on the back of bag in the same position.

❊ Attach a button to the centre of each reel.

❊ Sew the reels in place on the front of the bag, placing the top of each reel 5cm (2") down from the top of the bag and the outer edge of each reel 2.5cm (1") in from the side edge of the bag.

TIP: FOR AN EXTRA STRONG BAG, LINE IT WITH FABRIC AND BACK THE HANDLES WITH FABRIC.

STARSHIP
Blanket

This colourful blanket will brighten up a nursery or child's bedroom. The striking images incorporate all the elements of sci-fi space, stars, rockets and vivid colours. Each patch is knitted separately and sewn together at the end so it can be worked on easily without having to carry the whole blanket. The size can be adjusted by adding extra patches or taking them away. The techniques used include texture, cabling, intarsia, and beading.

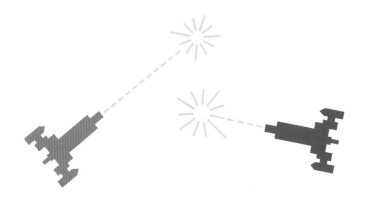

MATERIALS

YARN: Aran weight.

Shown here: Rowan Handknit Cotton (100% cotton; 93m (85yd)/50g): Turkish plum (A), 5 balls; rosso (red) (B) and Atlantic (C), 4 balls each; gooseberry (green) (D), Florence (orange) (E), cassis (pink) (F) and ochre (yellow) (G), 1 ball each.

NEEDLES: 4mm: straight.

HABERDASHERY: Pack of red beads, pack of blue beads, tapestry needle.

TENSION: 20 sts and 26 rows to 10cm (4") in St st.

FINISHED MEASUREMENT: Individual patch about (19.5cm (7¾") wide x 25.5cm (10") long. Completed blanket (16 patches) about 78.5cm (31") wide x 1m (40") long.

SPECIAL ABBREVIATIONS

C4F = slip 2 sts onto cn and hold in front of work, k2, k2 from cn

C6F = slip 3 sts onto cn and hold in front of work, k3, k3 from cn

C6B = slip 3 sts onto cn and hold in back of work, k3, k3 from cn

PATTERN Note

The border of each patch is worked in moss st for 5 rows at the top and bottom and 4 sts at each edge. Work chart from right to left on RS rows and from left to right on WS rows.

CABLE ROCKET 1

(Make 2)

Using shade A, cast on 39 sts.

ROW 1: *K1, p1 ; rep from * to last st, k1.

This row sets the moss st edging, rep the last row 4 more times.

NEXT ROW (WS): (K1, p1) twice, p31, (p1, k1) twice.

Keeping 4 sts at each outside in moss st, cont to work centre in St st throughout. Est Cable Rocket chart 1 as foll:

ROW 1 (RS): Using shade A [k1, p1] twice, k3. Start row 1 of chart 1, changing colours as indicated work 25 sts from chart, k3, [p1, k1] twice.

ROW 2 (WS): Using shade A [k1, p1] twice, p3, work row 2 of chart, p3, (p1, k1) twice.

Cont working 4 sts at each edge in moss st as est and centre in St st from the chart, changing colours and working cables as indicated until all 54 rows of Cable Rocket 1 chart pattern have been worked.

ROW 55 (RS): Using shade A, [K1, p1] twice, K31, [p1, k1] twice.

Rep Row 1 of moss st edging 5 times.

Cast off.

Cable Rocket 1

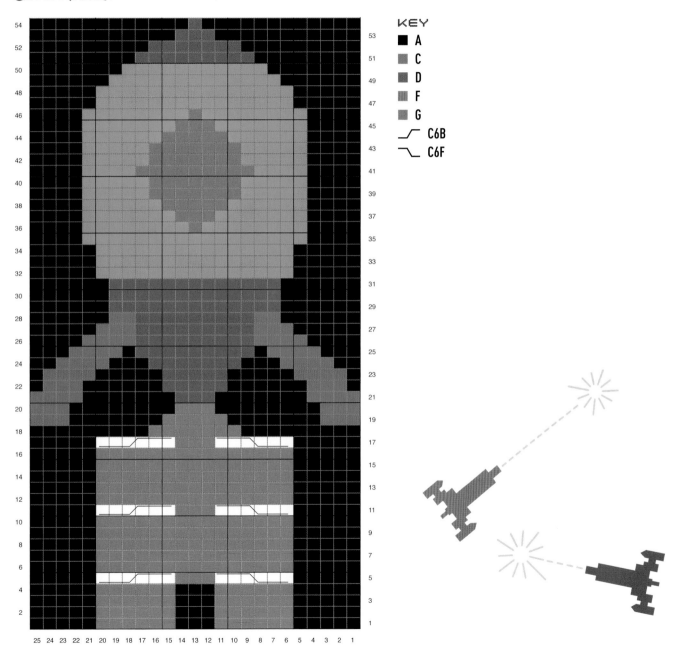

KEY

■	A
■	C
■	D
■	F
■	G
⌐	C6B
⌐	C6F

CABLE ROCKET 2

(Make 2)

Using shade A, cast on 39 sts.

ROW 1: *K1, p1; rep from * to last st, k1.

This row sets the moss st edging, repthe last row 4 more times.

NEXT ROW (WS): [K1, p1] twice, p31, [p1, k1] twice.

Keeping 4 sts at each outside edge in moss st, cont to work centre in St st throughout. Est Cable Rocket 2 chart as foll:

ROW 1 (RS): Using shade A, [k1, p1] twice, k6, changing colours as indicated work 18 sts from Cable Rocket 2 chart. Using shade A, k7, [p1, k1] twice.

ROW 2 (WS): Using shade A [k1, p1] twice, p7, work next row of Cable Rocket 2 chart. Using shade A, p6, [p1, k1] twice.

Cont working 4 sts at each edge in moss st as est and centre in St st from the chart changing colours and working cables as indicated until all 54 rows of Cable Rocket 2 chart pattern have been worked.

NEXT ROW (RS): [K1, p1] twice, k31, [p1, k1] twice.

Rep Row 1 of moss st edging 5 times.

Cast off.

STRIPE ROCKET 3

(Make 2)

Using shade A, cast on 37 sts.

ROW 1: *K1, p1; rep from * to last st, k1.

This sets the moss st edging, rep the last row 4 more times.

NEXT ROW (WS): [K1, p1] twice, p29, [p1, k1] twice.

Keeping 4 sts at each outside edge in moss st, cont to work centre in St st throughout. Est Stripe Rocket 3 as foll:

ROW 1 (RS): Using shade A, [k1, p1] twice, k4, changing colours as indicated work the 21 sts from Stripe Rocket 3 chart. Using shade A, k4, [p1, k1] twice.

ROW 2 (WS): Using shade A, [k1, p1] twice, p4, work next row of Stripe Rocket 3 chart. Using A, p4, (p1, k1) twice.

Cont working 4 sts at each edge in moss st as set and centre in St st from the Stripe Rocket 3 chart changing colours as indicated until all 54 rows of chart pattern have been worked.

NEXT ROW (RS): [K1, p1] twice, k29, [p1, k1] twice.

Rep Row 1 of moss st edging 5 times.

Cast off.

TIP: TO VARY THE DESIGN, CHANGE THE COLOURS ON EACH OF THE ROCKETS SO THAT THEY ARE IN SIX DIFFERENT SHADES AND WORK RANDOM STRIPES ON THE STRIPED PATCHES.

Cable Rocket 2

Stripe Rocket 3

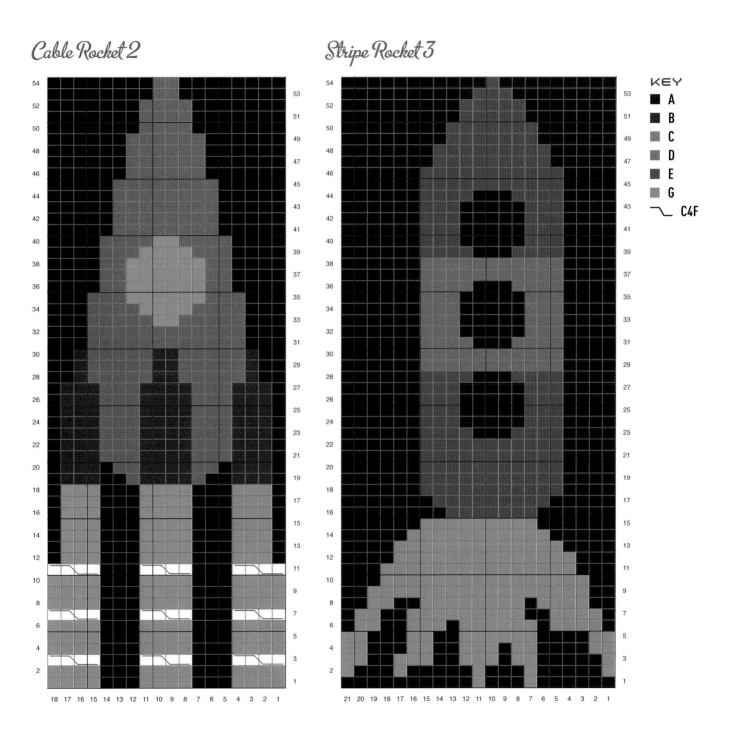

KEY

■	A
■	B
■	C
■	D
■	E
■	G
⌐__	C4F

BEADED STAR

(Make 1 using blue beads
and 1 using red beads)

Thread shade A with 80 beads.
Cast on 37 sts.

ROW 1: *K1, p1; rep from * to last st,
k1.

This sets the moss st edging, rep
the last row 4 more times.

NEXT ROW (WS): [K1, p1]
twice, p29, [p1, k1] twice.

Keeping 4 sts at each outside edge
in moss st, cont to work centre in
St st throughout. Est Beaded Star chart
(right) as foll:

ROW 1 (RS): Using shade A, [k1,
p1] twice, work the 29 sts from Beaded
Star chart. Using shade A, [p1, k1] twice.

ROW 2 (WS): Using shade A, [k1, p1]
twice, work next row of Beaded Star chart,
[p1, k1] twice.

Cont working 4 sts at each edge in
moss st as set and centre in St st
from the Beaded Star chart placing
beads as indicated until all 54 rows of
chart pattern have been worked.

NEXT ROW (RS): [K1, p1] twice,
K29, [p1, k1] twice.

Rep Row 1 of moss st edging 5 times.

Cast off.

Beaded Star

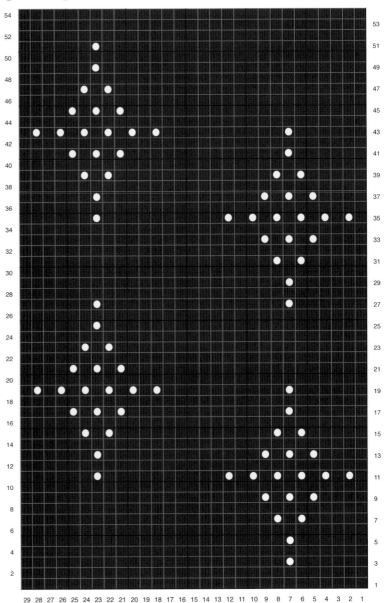

KEY

■ A   ○ BEAD (SEE TECHNIQUES)

TEXTURED STAR

(Make 1 using shade B and 1 using shade C)

Cast on 37 sts.

ROW 1: *K1, p1; rep from * to last st, k1.

This sets the moss st edging, rep the last row 4 more times.

NEXT ROW (WS): [K1, p1] twice, p29, [p1, k1] twice.

Keeping 4 sts at each outside edge in moss st, cont to work centre in St st throughout. Est Textured Star chart (right) as foll:

ROW 1 (RS): Using shade A, [K1, p1] twice, work the 29 sts from Textured Star chart, [p1, k1] twice.

ROW 2 (WS): Using shade A, [K1, p1] twice, work next row of chart. Using shade A, [p1, k1] twice.

Cont working 4 sts at each edge in moss st as set and centre in St st from the working textured pattern as indicated until all 54 rows of Textured Star chart pattern have been worked.

NEXT ROW (RS): Using shade A, [K1, p1] twice, k29, [p1, k1] twice.

Rep Row 1 of moss st edging 5 times.

Cast off.

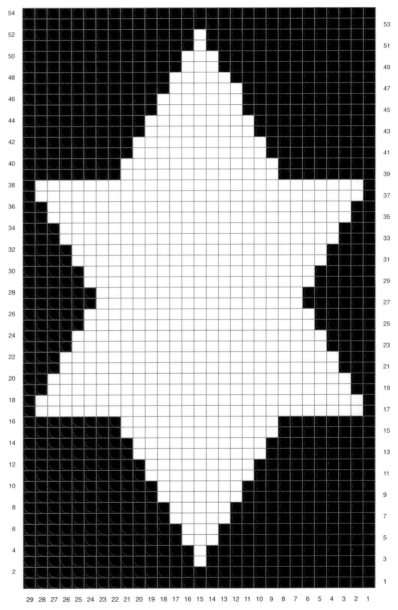

Textured Star

KEY
■ PURL ON RS, KNIT ON WS   □ KNIT ON RS, PURL ON WS

FINE STRIPE

(Make 4)

Using shade B cast on 37 sts.

ROW 1: *K1, p1; rep from * to last st, k1.

This sets the moss st edging, rep the last row 4 more times.

NEXT ROW (WS): [K1, p1] twice, p29, [p1, k1] twice.

Keeping 4 sts at each outside edge in moss st, cont to centre part in St st throughout. Est stripe sequence as foll:

ROW 1 (RS): E.

ROWS 2 & 3: B (rep these 2 rows after every contrast colour row).

ROW 4: F.

ROW 7: D.

ROW 10: C.

ROW 13: E.

ROW 16: D.

ROW 19: F.

ROW 22: C.

ROW 25: E.

ROW 28: C.

ROW 31: F.

ROW 34: D.

ROW 37: E.

ROW 40: F.

ROW 43: C.

ROW 46: D.

ROW 49: C.

ROW 52: F.

ROW 55: E.

ROW 56: B.

Using B rep Row 1 of moss st edging 5 times.

Cast off.

WIDE STRIPE

(Make 2)

Using shade A, cast on 37 sts.

ROW 1: *K1, p1; rep from * to last st, k1.

This sets the moss st edging, rep the last row 4 more times.

NEXT ROW [WS]: [K1, p1] twice, p29, [p1, k1] twice.

Keeping 4 sts at each outside edge in moss st, cont to work centre in St st throughout. Est stripe sequence as folls:

ROWS 1–4: C.

ROWS 5 & 6: B.

ROWS 7–10: C.

ROWS 11 & 12: G.

ROWS 13–16: C.

ROWS 17–20: A.

Rep Rows 1–20 once, then rep Rows 1–16 once.

ROW 57: A.

Cast off.

MAKING UP

✳ Block and press each patch and sew in all loose ends. Join each patch together in the sequence shown in the diagram.

Cable Rocket 1	Textured Star (B)	Stripe Rocket 3	Fine Stripe
Fine Stripe	Beaded Star (Blue)	Wide Stripe	Cable Rocket 2
Stripe Rocket 3	Wide Stripe	Beaded Star (Red)	Fine Stripe
Fine Stripe	Cable Rocket 2	Textured Star (C)	Cable Rocket 1

Conversion Charts

KNITTING NEEDLE CONVERSION

METRIC	UK	US
2	14	0
2.25	13	1
2.5	–	–
2.75	12	2
3	11	–
3.25	10	3
3.5	–	4
3.75	9	5
4	8	6
4.5	7	7
5	6	8
5.5	5	9
6	4	10
6.5	3	10 ½
7	2	–
7.5	1	–
8	0	11
9	00	13
10	000	15
12	–	17
15	–	19
20	–	35
25	–	50

CROCHET HOOK CONVERSION

METRIC	UK	US
2	14	–
2.25	13	B/1
2.5	12	–
2.75	–	C/2
3	11	–
3.25	10	D/3
3.5	9	E/4
3.75	–	F/5
4	8	G/6
4.5	7	7
5	6	H/8
5.5	5	I/9
6	4	J/10
6.5	3	K10 ½
7	2	–
8	0	L/11
9	00	M/13
10	000	N/15

INDEX